CAJUN VOCABULATION

GORDON J. VOISIN

iUniverse, Inc.
Bloomington

Cajun Vocabulation

The views expressed in this work are solely those of the author and do not necessarily reflect the views of the publisher, and the publisher hereby disclaims any responsibility for them.

iUniverse books may be ordered through booksellers or by contacting:

iUniverse
1663 Liberty Drive
Bloomington, IN 47403
www.iuniverse.com
1-800-Authors (1-800-288-4677)

Because of the dynamic nature of the Internet, any web addresses or links contained in this book may have changed since publication and may no longer be valid.

Any people depicted in stock imagery provided by Thinkstock are models, and such images are being used for illustrative purposes only.

Certain stock imagery © Thinkstock.

ISBN: 978-1-4620-0197-2 (sc)
ISBN: 978-1-4620-0198-9 (hc)
ISBN: 978-1-4620-0196-5 (ebk)

Printed in the United States of America

iUniverse rev. date: 12/13/2011

This book is dedicated to
Linest and Iona
Lillian
Matthew & Rick
Deanie, Eva, Simon, Mona, David, Kim & Nella
Tyler, Natasha
Aubrey Laine & Avery Lily
Allison
&
Tommy Lynn

Contents

Introduction ix

A Cajun is xi

Cajun Vocabulary 1

English to French 4

Cajun Surnames 71

Crazy Euphemisms 75

Anatomy of a Cajun 78

Nicknames 80

Colors 82

Insects and Things That Crawl 83

Animals and Four-legged Things 84

At What Time 85

Food, Beverages and Such 87

By the Numbers 89

Months of the Year 91

Days of the Week 92

Seafood 93

Things That Fly 94

Relations 95

Where 96

Slang and Silliness 97

Cajun Vocabulary Redux 113

French to English 115

About the Author 167

Introduction

Unless I miss my guess completely, we're on the verge of losing a unique part of our heritage, a heritage that the better part of the country doesn't know about, and fewer understand. We, the baby boomer generation, who are in our 60's understand Cajun French, and some of us speak it fairly well. My mom and dad spoke fluent Cajun French, but most of the time they did so to keep us from understanding what they were saying. They taught us the basics, but not much more. Being that my parents taught us little, we taught our children very little. They learned the cuss words, but not much else. Therefore, our next generation has very little incentive to speak or understand the language. It will have been almost dissipated from the regular Cajun populace by the next generation. Most of us subscribe to the "If you can't lick them, then join them" fraternity. In the annals of history we will be viewed as a people who let their language die a premature death, to be relegated to the dust bin of yesterday's uncertain sunset.

We, the baby boomers, shun the Cajun dialect that was spoken by our ancestors, possibly because we view it as being inferior and unsophisticated. Maybe we think, and are afraid, that others might think of us as being illiterate if we try to carry on the old time Cajun French language. Granted, our lifestyle and our language are unique but we will have failed to pass it on to out next generation.

Shame on us!

I'm proud to be a Cajun and this book is one man's attempt to preserve some of that uniqueness, an attempt to keep the spirit of the

Cajun lifestyle and language from extinction. This dictionary and its words all have one thing in common: They are woven into the tapestry of who we are as a people; an indigenous part of the lifestyle that we have learned, known and lived for the past 250 or so years. The elders taught me how to pronounce most of the words in this book. So the book follows the words of my elders, which means I speak the old-time Cajun French better than the current French that is being spoken today in some other places.

"Anh!"

Forty years ago that word captured my imagination and prompted me to write this book. The more I thought about it, the more the idea became viable. To me it seemed to be a small undertaking to try to put our language into print, a language that doesn't exist in any book form. I looked at it from the perspective that the book had to be written in such a way that anybody, say, someone from Northern Idaho, for example, could pronounce an approximation of what our words sound like. Was I wrong! As the years slipped by I kept revising and editing the body of my work, and what seemed to be a small project began to mushroom into a couple of thousand words. Therefore, I've divided into sections: English to French; lists of different things; Slang and Silliness, and French to English.

You need to remember that the Cajun French is a derivative of, a by-product of the Parisian French. This doesn't mean that it doesn't, by any means, infer that it is an inferior product. Standing upon it's own merits, Cajun French is a beautiful language in its own right, and should not be castigated because it doesn't meet the formal requisites of its mother language. The Cajun language in this book is based on my knowledge of the local usage, and from other sources, especially with the dozens of interviews with the elders in my community, those in the 70's, 80's and 90's and those now deceased. They taught me the old time Cajun French with all its innuendos and idiosyncrasies included. So, sit back, kick off your shoes, and try to speak Cajun French.

A Cajun is

Someone who will eat anything, (except Mountain Oysters) that won't eat him first.

Someone who would rather drink Dixie beer than sip champagne.

The one at the wedding wearing a tuxedo, a flower in his lapel, and also his brand new, too nuff, Dulac Rebokks (white shrimp boots).

The little girl who says "Snot me, sim diddit" when she broke something.

The only one who thinks that Mardi Graw ought to be a National Holiday.

The little boy who names his puppies Noo-noo, Pookie, Tee Chime and Alphonse.

The little girl who put an oyster sack by the Christmas tree. She knows that Sanny Claws can't put a bicycle in a little stocking.

The guy, who, if you ketch him wearing alligator shoes, then they're probably still moving.

The only species of human beans who don't talk with no accent (kind of like little Johnny's the only one in the band marching straight—all of the others are out of step).

The drunk who tells his wife that he came home late last night because an alligator ate his paddle and he had to paddle his pee-rogue with his hands to get home.

The lady up the bayou who hears on the radio that the Yankees sweep the White Sox and she thinks that it's funny that those Up-North people clean their socks with a broom.

The lady down the bayou who goes and wait by the mailbox because she heard on the television that the President is gonna' deliver a speech.

CAJUN VOCABULARY

The most important aspect of Cajun French is the rolling "R." To make a rolling "R" you flutter the tip of the tongue, upon the top of your palate and roll them. Try saying the words through, throat, three and throw, and you've just rolled four "R's." All R's are rolled in Cajun French, no matter where they occur. Without them it sounds too Americanized, which isn't altogether bad, but misses the point of what the Cajun French is meant to sound like.

The two most used syllables in the Cajun vocabulary are the "Anh" and "Onh." The "Anh" is made by taking the word "and," cutting the sound in half, stressing the "a" and eliminating the "d" sound. Try saying the words "animal" "can" and "ran," and you've pronounced the "Anh" sound. For the "Onh" sound you would say the word "on", and stretch the "o" sound and eliminate the "n" sound. Try the words "going" "gaunt" and "don't" and you've just pronounced the "Onh" sound. There are many other syllables that may be indigenous to the Cajun language. They are as follows:

Ah: As in bother, cot or yacht.
Ahl: As in Polly, collie or dolly.
Anh: As in ran, land and tan.
Arr: As in car, par or mar.
Aud: As in laud, bawdy or pawed.
Aw: As in saw, gnaw or father.
Awl: As in crawl, doll or ball.

Awm: As in ohm, home or roam.
Awsh: As in caution awash or squash.
Awz: As in clause, pause or cause.
Bah: As in bayou, bottle or bother.
Bawn: As in brawn, lawn or dawn.
Buh: As in butter, butt or barrage.
Cah or Kah: As in cog, college or collar.
Caw: As in paw, awe or saw.
Cawm: As in pome, loam or tome.
Cawt: As in ought, caught or thought.
Craw: As in paw, crawfish, or law.
Deux: As in heard, purple or pas de deux.
Dieu: As in girl, hurl or pearl.
Du: As in do, who or coo.
Duh: As in veranda, rough or dud.
Eau or Eaux: As in bureau, oh or know.
Ee: As in see, bee or three.
Eii: As in figure, ill or pill.
Ess: As in best, rest or mess.
Euh: As in pas de deux; burly or curly.
Eum: As in gum, sum or thumb.
Ev: As in heavy, levee or heaven.
Feuh: As in earth, early or burly.
Gah: As in God, mod or nod.
Guh: As in cut, but or rut.
Igg: As in big, fig or rig.
Jay: As in day way or hay.
Kah: As in cop, comic or pop.
Kai: As in lye, eye or pie.
Kawt: As in bought, sought or ought.
Kuhl: As in bull, wool or pull.
La: As in rah, ha, or lob.
Mott: As in cot, sot or what.
Muh: As in justice, just or must.
Nu: As in nuclear, noose or nude.
Nuh: A in nut, cut or dud.
Ohm: As in comb, home, or dome.

Oii: As in doing, booing or cooing.
Oin: As in coin, loin or join.
Onh: As in bone, gone or lone.
Ont or Awnt: As in want, haunt or taunt.
Oo: As in boot, toot or root.
Ought: As in caught, fought or moth.
Pah: As in pop, pocket, or faux pas
Poos: As in noose, moose or loose.
Rahl: As in collar, dollar or holler.
Roo: As in too, moo or coo.
Sah: As in cot, pah or hot.
Tood: As in you'd, rude or sued.
Uh: As in but, cut or hut.
Urr: As in purr, sir, or cur.
Uzz: As in does, buzz or fuzz.
Vii: As in vie, pie, or tie.
Waw: As in patois, wasp or squaw.
Yea: As in pay, way or say.
Yuh: As in hut, but, or cut.

English to French

A

A: An; anh.

Able: Kah-pop.

Aboard: Ah-bar.

Accident: Ox-see-donh.

Acid: Ah-sid.

Across from: Ah-poe-zay.

Additional: Oh-see.

Adhere: Call.

Adhered: Co-lay.

Advance: Ah-vawn-suh.

Advanced: Ah-vawn-say.

Affair: Ah-fair.

Affectionate term for a young boy: Neg.

Afraid: Purr.

African-American man: Neg, however this term is derogatory.

African-American female: Neg-ress, however this term is derogatory.

After: Ah-pray.

After noon: Ah-pray-me-dee.

After somebody: Pod-duh-yair.

After while: Donh-an-alonh.

Again: Onh-car.

Against (to go): Ah-pause.

Agreeable: Ah-gray-yobb.

Aground: A-schway.
Ahead: Prawm-yair.
Alcoholic drink: Bwaw-sonh; co-loy.
Alike: Mam-shawz.
All: Toot; too.
All around: Tool-tour.
Alligator: Kai-monh.
All over: Pot-too; too-pot-too.
Allow: Kit; less.
All the time: Tool-tonh.
Almost: Ah-pray-pray; press-kuh; prawsh.
Alone: Sull; monh-sull.
A long time: Lonh-tonh.
Already: Day-jah.
Also: Oh-see.
Always: Tool-tonh.
Ambition: Ess-pwarr.
Ammunition: Cot-toosh.
Anchor: Onk; grop-anh.
Angel: Onj.
Anger: Co-lair.
Anger (to): Shawk.
Angered: Show-kay.
Angry (too make): A-show-kay; chu-rouge; fah-shay.
Animal: Annie-moe.
Another: An-ought.
Another thing: An-ought-shawz.
Another time: An-ought-fwaw.
Answer: Ray-pawn.
Answered: Ray-pawn-du.
Ants: Frawm-mee.
Anyone: No-pote-tuh-kell.
Anything: No-pote-tuh-key.
A-pang: A pin to hold clothes on a clothes line.
Apiece: Pyess.
Apparently: Onh-dee-ray.
Appearance: Ah-pah-rawnce.

5

Appears as though: Sawm.
Apple: Pawm; pome.
Apprentice: Ah-prawn-tee.
Approach: Ah-prawsh.
Approached: Ah-pro-shay.
April: Ah-vreel.
Argue: Oh-stin; diss-put.
Argued: Oh-steen-nay.
Argument: Shawm-my; diss-put.
Arm: Bra.
Around: Oh-tour.
Arrange: Ah-roan-juh.
Arranged: Ah-roan-jay.
Arrive: Ah-riv.
Arrived: Ah-ree-vay.
Arrogant: Fawn-chock.
As: Cawm.
ASAP: Toot-sweet.
Ascend: Gramp.
Ascended: Gramp-pay.
As good: Bawn.
Ashore: Ah-tair.
Ask: Udd-mawn.
Asleep: Darr.
Asphyxiate: A toof.
Asphyxiated: A-too-fay.
Aspiration: Ess-pwarr.
Ate: Mawn-jay.
Athlete's foot: God-noo-shett.
At one time: Pod-duh-an-fwaw.
At sea: Ah-la-mair.
Attach: Ah-tosh.
Attached: Ah-tosh-shay.
Attempt: Ah-say-yuh.
Attempted: Ah-say-yea.
Attic: Gran-yea.
Attitude: Ah-bee-tood.

Audacity: Too-pay.
August: Ah-woo.
Aunt: Taunt.
Aunt (little): Tee-taunt.
Autumn: Oh-taum.
Awaken: Ray-vay-yea.
Aware: Ah-pair-sue.
A way: Monh-yair.
Awful: Thriss.
Awkward: Froo-froo; gawsh.
Awn-too-rodge: A wall.

B

Baby: Bay-bay.
Back (in): Onh-nod-yair.
Back (the): Doe.
Backward: Ah-lawn-vair.
Bad: Moe-vay; moll.
Bad smell: Pue.
Bad squall: Oh-rodge; tonh-pet.
Bait: Ah-pah.
Ball: Plaut.
Bamboo: Row-zoe.
Banana: Bah-nawn.
Bank: Bonk.
Bare: Nu.
Bare foot: Nu-pyea.
Bark: Jop.
Barked: Jop-pay.
Basket: Ponh-yea.
Bass (fish): Thritt-vair.
Bastard: Bah-tard; onh-fawnh-de-goss.
Bath (to take a): Ban-yea.
Bath room: Shawm-ah-banh.
Bath towel: Sair viet.
Battered: Cob-oh-say.
Battery: Bah-three.
Battle: Bah-tie. Also, a Cajun card game.

Beans: Ben.
Beard: Bob.
Beast: Bay-tie.
Beaten: Foo-tu.
Beat up: Cob-oh-say.
Beautiful: Bow.
Beautiful woman: Joe-lee; bell.
Because: Poss-kuh.
Became aware of: Ah-pair-sue.
Become accustomed to: Ah-bue-tway.
Bed: Lee.
Bed room: Shawm-ah-lee.
Beets: Bay-thrav.
Before: Onh-nah-vonh.
Before noon: Ah-vonh-mee-dee.
Began: Cawm-onh-say.
Begin: Cawm-awnse.
Beginner: Ah-prawn-tee.
Behind (in back of): Onh-nod-yair.
Behind (position): Dan-yea.
Behind (the): Dair-yair; chu.
Behind the back: Onh-kah-shett.
Beignet: Ban-yea.
Belch: Rawt.
Belched: Row-tay.
Bell: Clawsh.
Belly: Vaunt.
Belly button: Nawm-bree.
Belonging to us: Naught; pot-chanh.
Belt (a): San-tour.
Bent: Crawsh; crow-shay.
Be rid of: Day-fair.
Bet (to): Pah-ree.
Better: Pleu-bonh; muh-yurr.
Between: Ont.
Big event: Coo.
Big Female: Grown.

Big male: Gronh.
Billfold: Pawt-mawn-nay.
Bill (money): Bee-yea.
Biloxi: Bay-lux-see.
Bird: Zwaw-zoe.
Birth: A-nay.
Birthday: Fett.
Biscuit: Biss-quee.
Bit: Mord-du.
Bite: Mord.
Bitten: Mord-du.
Black: Nwarr.
Blackberry dumplings: Poe-ten.
Black drum (fish): Taum-bow.
Black mullet (fish): Muy-nwarr.
Black pepper: Pwaw-vuh.
Blade: Lawm.
Blanket: Blonh-kett.
Bleed: Sanh-yuh.
Bleeding: Sanh-yea.
Bless: Blay-say.
Blessed: Bee-nee.
Blew (the wind): Vonh-tay.
Blister: Onh-poul.
Bloat: Gonh-flay.
Bloated: Gonf.
Block: Blauk.
Blocked: Blow-kay.
Blond: Blawn.
Blood: Sonh.
Boat: Bah-tow.
Boat (broken down): Day-poo-yuh; day-pooi.
Boil (a): Clew.
Boil (to): Boo-yuh.
Boiled: Boo-yea.
Boisterous: Bosk-you-luzz.
Boll-yea: A broom. Also to sweep.

Bolt: Boo-lonh

Bones: Aw-suh.

Book: Liv.

Boots: Bought.

Border: Bode-durr.

Born: A-nay.

Borrowed: Onh-pray-tay.

Bother (to): Onh-bet; jan; shah-grin.

Bothered: Onh-bay-tay; jan nay; shah-gree-nay.

Bottom: Fonh.

Boudin: Cajun style sausage; boo-danh.

Bought: Osh-tay.

Bourre' (a Cajun card game): Boo-ray.

Bow (the front of a boat): A-thrauv.

Bowl: Ball.

Box: Bwett.

Boy: Boog; gar-sonh.

Braggart: Vaunt-turr.

Brain: Sair-vell.

Brave: Brauv.

Bread: Panh.

Break (to): Koss.

Breakfast: Day-jan-nay.

Breasts: Tay-ten.

Breath: Soof.

Breathe: Soo-flay.

Breeze: Brizz.

Bright: Bree-yont.

Brilliant: Bree-yont.

Bring: Onh-man.

Bring back: Ohm-nay.

Broke: Koss-say.

Broken: Kah-say.

Broken down: Day-brang-gay.

Broken down car: Shah-rett.

Brother: Frair.

Brother-in-law: Bow-frair.

Brought: Ohm-nay; roam-nay.

Brush: Braw suh.

Bucket: Syoe.

Buddy: Pod-nah.

Buggy: Bow-gay.

Building (carpenters do this): Bah-tear.

Building (a): Bah-tiss.

Built: Bah-tee.

Bull: Buff; tow-row.

Bull-frog: Wah-wah-ronh.

Buoy: Bway.

Burial: Onh-tair-monh.

Buried: Onh-tay-ray.

Burn (a): Brew-lure.

Burn (to): Brewl.

Burned: Brew-lay.

Burned food: Gree-yea.

Burnt: Bruel-lay.

Bury: Onh-tair.

Bushel: Ponh-yea.

Busted: Day-fawn-say.

Busybody: Ess-peonh-nurr.

Butt: Fonh; pay-tard.

Butter: Burr.

Butterbeans: Fev-plot.

Butterfly: Pop-ee-yonh.

Butter flyer: Pope-yair-urr.

Butterfly nets: Pope-yair.

Buttocks: Fess.

Button: Boot-onh.

Buy (to): Jet.

By myself: Monh-sull.

By the seat of the pants: Fawned-key-lawt.

C

Cabbage: Shoe.

Cable (nautical term): Cob.

Cajun card games: Boo-ray, peed-row, Bah-tie, Sasquatch; Screw your neighbor.

Cajun hutch: Gar-mawn-jay (literally look, food).

Cajun sideboard: Gar-mawn-jay.

Cake: Got-oh.

Cake (small, one layer): Gah-lett; ban-yea.

Calf: Voe.

Call: Ah-pell.

Called: Ah-play.

Calmed down: Coll-mee.

Calming down: Coll-meer.

Came: Mnu.

Came-down: Day-sawn-du.

Came in: Roan-tray.

Camel: Shom-oh.

Came near: Ah-pro-shay.

Came out: Soat-tee.

Can (I or You): Kah-pop.

Canal: Con ahl.

Canal (for trappers): Tran-oss.

Cancer: Cawn-sair.

Candle: Shawn-dell.

Candy: Cawn-dee.

Cane: Cawn.

Cane reed: Kah-nush.

Can't: Pah-pah.

Cap: Koss; shop-oh.

Capable: Kah-pop.

Capitol: Cop-ee-tahl.

Caprice: Kah-priss.

Capsize: Cop-poe-tay.

Captain: Cop-ee-tan.

Car: Sharr.

Card: Cot.

Card games (Cajun): Boo-ray, bah-tie, peed-row Sasquath and Screw Your Neighbor.

Careless: Froo-froo.

Carpenter: Share-pawn-turr.
Carpentry (is doing): Share-pawn-tay.
Carpentry work: Share-pawnt.
Carried: Port-tay.
Carrot: Kah-rawt.
Carry: Part.
Carryings on: Shod-odd.
Cart: Shah-rett.
Cartridges: Cot-toosh.
Car window: Vitt.
Case: Kess.
Cast net: A-preeve-yea.
Cat: Shah.
Catch: Ah-throp.
Catechism: Kah-tay-shiss.
Catfish: Barb-bue.
Catholic: Cot-oh-lick.
Cattle: Annie-moe; bay-tie; vawsh.
Caught: Ah-throp-pay; onh pawn-yea.
Caught (got): Prawn.
Cauldron: Showed-yair.
Caulk: Goll-fett.
Caulked: Goll-fay-tay.
Cedar: Said.
Celebrate: Sell-a-bray.
Celery: Sell-rhee.
Cemetery: Seem-me-tyair.
Center: Meel-yeuh.
Chafed: A-show-fay.
Chagrin: Shah-grin.
Chagrined: Shah-gree-nay.
Chain: Shan.
Chair: Shezz.
Chamber pot: Pah-chawm.
Chance: Shawn-suh.
Chandelier: Shawn-dill-yea.
Change (money): A-shawn-juh.

Change (to): Shawn-juh.
Changed: Shawn-jay.
Changed ends: Vee-rayed-boot.
Changed residence: Day-low-jay.
Chase: Coor-say.
Chase (the): Ah-la-coose.
Chasing: Pod-duh-yair.
Chatter: Rah-dawt.
Cheap: Bawn-mahr-shay.
Cheese: Frawm-modge.
Cherished: Share.
Chest of drawers: She-fawn-war.
Chew: Shick.
Chewed: Shee-kay.
Chicanery: Shee-cawn-ree.
Chicken: Pool.
Chicken (Fryer): Voe-lye.
Chicken coop: Peeve-yea.
Chicken pox: Pee-caught.
Chicken yard: Poo-lye-yea.
Chiffonier: She-fawn-war.
Child: Onh-fonh; pee-tee.
Children: Daze-onh-fonh.
Chills: Free-sonhs.
Chilly: Fray.
Chimney: Sheem-nay.
Chin: Monh-tonh.
Chinese: Sheen-waw.
Chocolate: Shock-oh-la.
Choke: A-throng-glay.
Choose: Shwaw.
Choosy: Day-fay-sill.
Chose: Shwaw-zee.
Christmas: Chrees-muss.
Church: A-glizz.
Church collection: Kett.
Cigar: See-gahr.

Cigarette: See-gah-ritt.
Circular: Ronh.
Cistern: See-tan.
City: Vill.
Claw (a): Panse.
Claw (to): Grah-fee-yea.
Clean (to): Nay-twoy.
Clean (to be): Prawp.
Clean (wipe): Swee-yea.
Cleaned: Nay-twoy-yea.
Clear: Clair.
Cleared up: A-clair-see.
Climb: Gramp.
Climbed: Gram-pay.
Clock: Pawn-duel.
Close (to): Fram.
Close (to be): Pray.
Closed: Fram-may.
Cloth: A-toff.
Clothes: Lange.
Clothes basket: Pawn-yea-ah-lange.
Clover: Threff.
Coat: Cop-oh.
Coating of filth: Chrutt.
Cobwebs: Filled-nan-yea.
Cocky: Fawn-chock.
Coffee: Kah-fay.
Coffee pot: Greg-ah-kah-fay.
Coffin: Sair-cuy.
Coins: A-shawn-juh.
Colander: Cool-war.
Cold (is): Fraw.
Collection: Co-leck-syonh.
Collection (in church): Kett.
College: Co-ledge.
Color: Coo-lurr.
Come: Vyanh.

Come (will): Vom-near.
Come down: Day-sawn.
Common: Cawm-unh.
Communion: Cawm-mee-yonh.
Companion: Ah-mee; pod-nah.
Company (a): Cawm-pawn-yee.
Company (visitors): Cawm-pawn-yee.
Compartment to ice shrimp: Coll.
Compass: Cawm-pah.
Complain: Plan-yea.
Complaining: Ah-pray plan-yea.
Completely crazy: Foo-net.
Condom: Cop-ought.
Constipated: Cawn-stee-pay.
Contingent upon: Dah-bar.
Continue: Cawn-tee-noo.
Continuing: Too-jour.
Contraption: Onh-grew-shodd.
Cook (to): Quee.
Cooked: Quee.
Cooking: Queer.
Cooking pot: Showed-yair.
Cool: Fray.
Cop: Oh-feece-yea.
Copper: Quiv.
Corn: My-yee.
Corner: Quanh.
Correct: Co-rheck.
Corrosion, (usually of rust): Roo-yea.
Couch: So-fah.
Cough: Toose.
Coughed: Too-say.
Could: Foe-rah; poo-vay.
Count: Cawnt.
Counted: Cawn-tay.
Counter (in the kitchen or restaurant): Cawnt-war.
Courage: Coo-rodge; curr.

Court bouillon: Coo-bee-yawn.
Cousin: Cooz-anh.
Cover: Coo-vair.
Covering: Coo-vair-tour.
Cow: Vawsh.
Crab: Crobb.
Crab (hermit): Too-loo-loo.
Crab (soft shelled): Crobb-mall.
Crack: Crock.
Cravat: Crah-vott.
Crawfish: A-cray-viss.
Crawl: Thran-nay.
Craze: Chrizz.
Crazy female: Fall.
Crazy male: Foo.
Cream: Cram.
Credit: Cray-dee.
Creosote board: Mod-ree-yea.
Cricket: Kree-kett.
Cried: Cree-yea; jull-lay; pleur-ray.
Crime: Krimm.
Criminal: Cree-mee-nahl.
Crippled: Flee-jay.
Crocodile: Co-co-dree.
Crooked: Crawsh.
Cross: Craw.
Croup: Co-leush.
Crumb: Gree-yoe.
Crust: Chrutt.
Crutch: Bay-key-yuh.
Cry: Jull.
Crying: La-lamb.
Cry out: Cree.
Cried out: Cree-yea.
Cucumber: Co-cawm.
Cup: Tah-suh.
Cure: Gay-rear.

Cured: Gay-ree.
Curls (in the hair): Boo-klett.
Curse (a Cajun hex): Gree-gree.
Curse (to): Jurr.
Cursed: Jew-day; moo-dee.
Curtain: Ree-doe.
Cut: Coup.
Cylinder: See-lan.
Cylinder oil: Wrill duh-see-lan.
Cypress: Sip.

D

Daddy: Pair.
Damage: Mah sock; dawm-odge.
Damaged: Mah sock-ray; dawm-ah-jay.
Damned: Moo-dee.
Dance (a): Bahl.
Dance (to): Dawnce.
Dandruff: Poe-mort.
Danger: Dawn-jay.
Dark: Nwarr.
Day (a): June-nay.
Day after tomorrow: Lawn-manh.
Daytime: Jour.
Dead: Mort.
Dear: Share.
Debris (from the tide): Roam-ah-see.
Decayed: Poo-ree.
December: Day-sawm.
Decide: Day-sid.
Decided: Day-see-day.
Deckhand (on a boat): Mott-low.
Defend: Day-fawn.
Defense: Day-fawn suh.
Deformed: Ess-throw-pyea.
Delicate: Day-lee-cot; frah geel.
Delicious: Day-lease-yuh.
Deliver: Day-liv.

Delivered: Day-leave-ray.
Dented: Crow-she.
Dentist: Dawn-tiss.
Dentures: Rah-teal-yea.
Depend on: Day-pawn.
Derriere: Chu; fonh.
Descend: Day-sawn.
Descended: Day-sawn-du.
Desire: Day-zear; onh-vee.
Desire (to): Day-zear.
Desired: Day-zee-ray.
Destroy: A-cree-blay.
Devil: Dyobb.
Devoured: Day-voe-ray.
Diaper: Coosh.
Dictionary: Deek-syonh-nair.
Did: Fay.
Did put away: Roam-ah-say.
Did wrong: Moll.
Die: Crev.
Died: Cray-vay.
Dig: Fooi.
Digger: Foor-guy-yurr.
Digging: Foo-yea.
Dinner: Dee-nay.
Dip net: Cod-lay.
Dirt: Tair; chross; poos-yair.
Dirtied: Sah-lee.
Dirty: Sahl.
Dirty (getting): Sah-leer.
Dirty (got): Sah-lee.
Disabled: Ess-throw-pyea.
Discharged: Day-share-jay.
Disgrace: Daze-awn-urr.
Dishes: Vay-sell.
Disheveled: Moll-ah-jawn-tray.
Dishonor: Daze-awn-urr.

Dish towel: Sair-viet.
Dismantle: Ah-bott; day brang-gay.
Dispute: Diss-put.
Disputed: Diss-pew-tay.
Distant: Deese-tawn-suh.
Distant past: Lonh-tonh-pah-say.
Distasteful: Zee-rob; zear.
Ditch: Con-ahl.
Dive: Plawn-jay.
Divorce: Day-varce.
Dizzy (to feel): Kah-goo; fie.
Do (to): Fay.
Do (will): Fair.
Doctor: Doak-turr.
Doer: Fay-zurr.
Dog (female): Shyan.
Dog (male): Shyanh.
Door: Pawt.
Dose (of medicine): Dawss.
Doubled: Doob.
Doubt: Doot.
Doubted: Doo-tay.
Dove: Plawn-jay.
Down: Pot-air.
Down the bayou: Onh-bah.
Dozen: Doo-zan.
Drag: Thran.
Dragging: Thran-nay.
Drank: Bue.
Drawer: Teer-war.
Drawers (underwear): Cawn-sonh.
Dream (a): Rev.
Dreamed: Ray-vay.
Dreaming: Ah-pray-ray-vay.
Dress (a): Raub.
Dressed up: Ah-bee-yea.
Dried: Shay-say.

Drink(to): Bwaw.
Drinking: Bwarr.
Drizzling: Gran-noss say.
Drool: Bah-vay.
Drop: Shop.
Dropped: A-shop-pay.
Drum (a saltwater fish): Tawm-bow.
Drunk (is): Soo.
Drunk (was): Soo-lay.
Drunkard: Eve-ronh-yuh.
Dry (is): Seck.
Dry (to): Shess.
Drying: Shay-say.
Duck (a): Con-narr.
Duck with an awkward flight: Zanh-zanh.
Duck of the water: Pool-doe.
Dug: Foo-yea; foor-guy-yea.
Dummy: Donh-yonh.
Dump: Cop-ought.
Dumped over: Cop-oh-tay.
Dust: Poos-yair.

E

Each: Pyess; shock.
Each one: Shock-a-yan.
Ear: Oar-aye.
Early: Bawn-urr.
Earned: May-ree-tay.
Earth: Tair.
Ease: Ezz.
East: Ess.
Easter: Pock.
Easy: A-zay; samp.
Easy going: Ah-gray-yobb.
Eat: Day-jan-a; mawnge.
Eating: Mawn-jay.
Edge: Bode-durr.
Eel: Awn-ghee.

Egg: Uff.
Eight: Witt.
Eighteen: Deez-witt.
Eighty: Cot-ruh-vanh (literally four twenties).
Elastic: La-stick.
Electricity: Ee-leck-three-see-tay.
Eleven: Onze.
Embarrass: Haunt.
Embarrassed: Onh-bah-rah-say.
Embraced: Onh-bross-say.
Empty (to): Vee-day.
Empty (to be): Vidd.
Encrusted: Crew-tay.
End: Boot; fanh.
Enemy: Ill-me.
Engaged: Onh-gah-jay.
Engaged (to be married): Pray-tawn-du.
English: Awn-glay.
Enough: Ah-say.
Entangle: May-lay.
Entanglement: May-lodge-monh.
Enter: Rawnt.
Entered: Rawn-tray.
Entire thing: Toot.
Envelope: Onh-vlaup.
Equal: A-goll.
Escape: A-shop.
Escaped: A-shop-pay.
Especially: Ess-pree.
Even: Sur-monh.
Even (to be): A-goll.
Evening: Ah-pray-mee-dee.
Event: Ah-fair.
Everything: Too.
Everywhere: Pot-too.
Exact: Jhuss; ex-zock.
Exactly: Ex-zock-tee-monh.

Examination: Ex-zonh-me-nay.

Examine: Ex-zonh-men.

Excited: Ex-see-tay.

Excitement: Ex-see-tah-syonh.

Excuse (an): Ex-cuzz.

Excuse (to): Ex-you-zay.

Expel gas: Pet.

Expelled gas: Pay-tay.

Explain: Ex-plick.

Explained: Ex-plea-kay.

Exploded: Ex-ploze-zay.

Exquisite: Ex-kwee-zay.

Expenditures: Day-pawn-suh.

Extinguish: A-tanh.

Extinguished: A-tan.

Extra: Ex-trah.

Extremely stupid person: Goof-onh.

Eye brows: Sue-see.

Eye: Uh-yuh.

Eye glasses: Lee-net.

Eyes: Zeuh.

F

Fabric: A-toff.

Face: Fee-gurr.

Faces (making): Free-moose.

Factory: Fock-three.

Fad: Crizz.

Faint (feeling): Cah-goo; fie.

Faint (to): Avon-weer.

Fainted: Avon-wee.

Fair: Jhuss.

Fairly okay: Sah-vah.

Fall (the) (A season): Oh-tawm.

Fall (to): Tawm.

False teeth: Rah-teal-yea.

Famished: Day-voe-ray.

Fan: A-vawn-tie.

Far: Lwanh.
Fast (was): Vitt.
Father: Pair.
Fatigue: Fah-tick.
Fatigued(to be): Fah-tee-cawnt.
Fatigued (was): Fah-tee-kay.
Fat female: Grah; gross.
Fat male: Grow; gronh.
Fat Tuesday: Mod-dee-grah.
Faucet: Roe-bee-nay.
Fault: Fought.
February: Fev-ree-yea.
Feel: Sont.
Feet (to walk with): Pyea.
Fell: Tawm-bay.
Fell asleep: Onh-door-me.
Felt: Sonh-tay.
Felt-faint: Fie; kah-goo.
Female: Fawm; fee-mell.
Female dog: Shyan.
Fence: Bahr-yair.
Ferocious: Fay-ross.
Field: Shomp.
Fifteen: Cans.
Fifty: San-cont.
Fifty cents: San-cont-sue.
Fight: Bah-tie; diss-put; shawm-my.
Figure: Fee-gurr.
File (a): Lim.
Fill: Roam-plea.
Fillet: Fee-lay.
Filling: Roam-pleer.
Filth: Chross; chroot.
Filthy: Crew-tay.
Final: Dan-yea.
Finger: Dwaw.
Find: Throove.

Finicky: Pot-tee-cool-yea.
Finish: Fee-knee.
Finished: Foo-tu.
Finishing: Fee-near.
Fire: Feuh.
Fireplace: Foy-yea.
First (is): Prawm-yea.
First (was): Prawm-yair.
Fish (a): Pwaw-sonh.
Fish (to): Pesh.
Fisherman: Pay-shurr.
Fishing: Pay-shay.
Fishing cork: Boosh-onh.
Fishing rod or pole: Ling.
Fit (to have a): Crizz.
Five: Sank.
Five cents: San-soo.
Flame: Flawm.
Flannel material: Dome-met.
Flat: Plot.
Flatter: Flot-ooze.
Flea: Puss.
Flew: Voe-lay.
Float: Flawt.
Floated: Flow-tay.
Floor: Plonh-shay.
Flounder (fish): Plea.
Flour: Fah-rin.
Flour sauce: Roo.
Flower: Flurr.
Fly (a): Moosh.
Fly (to): Vall.
Fly catcher: Gob-moosh.
Fog: Brew-yodd.
Fold: Ploy.
Folded: Ploy-yea.
Follow: Swee.

Following: Sweer.
Food: Mawn-jay.
Foolish: Bet; dah-lah.
Foolishness: Bay-tizz; coo-yawn-odd.
Foot (a): Pyea.
Foot (the): Pot.
Forage: Foor-guy-yea.
Forager: Foor-guy-urr.
Force: Farce.
Forehead: Fronh.
Forest: Foe-ray.
Forgave: Par-donh-nay.
Forget: Oh-blee-yuh.
Forgive: Par-donh.
Forgot: Oh-blee-yea.
Fork: Four-shett.
Forty: Kah-ront.
Forward: Ah-vawnse.
Fought: Bah-tee; diss-put-tay; shawm-my-yea.
Foul: Moo-dee.
Found: Throove-vay.
Four: Cot.
Fourteen: Cot-awes.
Fragile: Frah-geel.
Freckled: Bah-zonh-nay.
Free (to): La-shay.
Freeze: Jhlay.
French: Fronh-say.
French duck: Kah-narr-fronh-say.
French toast: Panh-pad-du; (literally, "lost bread").
Frequent: Fray-cawnt.
Fresh: Fray.
Fresh water fish: Socka-lay; pah-tah-sah; thritt-vair.
Friday: Vaunt-ruh-dee.
Fried: Free.
Friend: Ah-mee; pod-nah.
Frog-(little green one): Good-noii.

Frown: Free-moose.
Fruit: Froo.
Frying pan: Pwall.
Full: Plan.
Fully crazy: Crock-been; foo-net.
Fun: De-shwaw.
Funeral: Onh-tair-monh.
Funnel: Rotten-war.
Furniture: May-nodge.
Fuss: Diss-put.
Fussed: Diss-pue-tay.
G
Gained weight: Onh-gray-say.
Gamble: Gamm-blay.
Gambler: Gamm-blur.
Game: Gimm.
Garden: Jod-danh.
Garlic: Lye.
Gasoline: Gozz.
Gave: Dawn-nay.
Get loose: A-shop.
Get smaller: Rop-tiss.
Get use to: Ah-bue-tway.
Gigolo: Mock-crow.
Gill net (seine): Throwm-my.
Girl (little): Teet-fee-yuh.
Give: Dawn.
Gizzard: Geez-yea.
Glad: Conh-taunt.
Glass (a): Vair.
Glass (window): Vitt.
Glasses (to see with): Lee-net.
Globe: Glaub.
Glove: Gonh.
Glutton: Day-fawn-say.
Gnats: Brew-low.
Go (to): Vah.

Go (will): Ah-lay.

Go ahead: Ah-vawnse.

Go and get: Share-shay.

Goat: Cob-ree.

Goblet: Go-blay.

God: Luh-Bawn-Dieu.

Godfather: Pah-ranh.

Godmother: Mah-ran; nuh-nan.

Go forward: Ah-vawnse.

Gold: L'orr.

Gone: Pot-tea.

Good (no): Moo-dee.

Good looking: Bow.

Good Lord: Bawn-Dieu.

Good sense: Bawn-ess-pree.

Goose: Zwaw.

Goose bumps: Free-sonh.

Got away: A-shop-pay.

Got colder: Rah-fraud-deer.

Got in the way of: Blow-kay.

Got loose: A-shop-pay.

Go to bed: Coo-shay.

Got smaller: Rop-tee-say.

Government: Goo-vair-nuh-monh.

Governor: Goo-vair-nurr.

Graduate (to): Grodd-you-way.

Grandfather: Groan-pair.

Grandmother: Groan-mare.

Grapnel: Grop-anh.

Grass (plural): Daze-abb.

Gravel: Grah-vwaw.

Grease: Gress.

Greased: Gray-say.

Greediness: Goor-monh-dizz.

Greedy: Goor-monh.

Green: Vair.

Green trout (bass): Thritt-vair.

Grew: Poo-say.
Greif: La-pan.
Groceries: Gross-ree.
Ground meat: Vyawn-moo-lay.
Grow (to): Poos.
Guarantee: Gah-ronh-tee.
Gumbo fillet: Ghom-bow-fee-lay.
Gum: Ghom.
Gums: Jhonh-siv.
Gun: Few-zee.
Gut (the): Thrip.
Gutted: A-three-pay.
Gutter: Dahl.

H

Habit: Ah-bee-tood.
Had: Ah-vay.
Hair: Pwell; schfeux.
Hairy: Pwell-ooze.
Half: Moe-chay.
Half an hour: An-dee-mee-yurr.
Ham: Jhom-bonh.
Hammer (a): Mott-toe.
Hammer (to): Tah-pawsh.
Hammering: Top-poe-shay.
Handicapped: Flee-jay; ess-throw-yea.
Handkerchief: Moosh-war.
Handle: Mawnsh.
Hang: Pawn.
Happen: Ah-riv.
Happened: Ah-ree-vay.
Happening (a): Coo.
Happy: Conh-taunt.
Hard: Durr.
Hardhead: Tet-durr.
Has: Ah.
Hat: Shop-oh.
Hatch cover to where shrimpers ice shrimp: Ponno.

Hatchet (A big one): Hawsh.
Hatchet: (A small one); Koss-tet.
Have (to): Ah-war.
He: Ee; lwee.
Head: Tet.
Headache: Moll-duh-tet.
Heal: Gay-rear.
Healed: Gay-ree.
Hear: Ah-tawn.
Heard: Ah-tawn-du.
Heart: Cur.
Heart trouble: Moll-ah-deed-curr.
Heat: Shah-lurr.
Heated: Shaud.
Heater: Ray-show.
Heavy: Lourd.
Held: Chan.
Hell: Lawn-fair.
Help: Ed.
Helped: A-day.
Helping: Ah-pray-a-day.
Hemorrhoids: A-more-witt.
Her: Ell.
Here: Ee-see.
Herself: Ell-mam.
Hex (Cajun style): Gree-gree.
Hiccups: Low-kay.
Hidden: Onh-kah-shett; kah-shay.
Hide: Kawsh.
High (is): Hoe.
High (was): Hawt.
Him: Ee; lwee.
Himself: Lwee-mam.
Hip: Hawnsh.
Hire: Onh-gah-jay.
His: Sonh.
History: Hees-twarr.

Hit (did): Tah-pay.
Hit(to): Fly-yea.
Hit lightly: Top.
Hit really hard: Co-lay.
Hoarse: Onhr-way.
Hogshead cheese: Jhlay.
Hold: Chanh.
Holding: Chan.
Hole: Through.
Holiday: Fet.
Holler: What you yell for a minor hurt; aye yie.
Holler: What you yell for a major hurt; aye-yuh-yie.
Holy: Be-knee.
Home: May-zone.
Honest: Onh net.
Honesty: Vay-ree-tay; awn-net.
Honey: Myell.
Honey bee: Moosh-ah-myell.
Hook (a): Ohm-sonh.
Hooked: Crow-she; crawsh.
Horn: Corn.
Horse: Schfawl.
Horsepower: Shuh-voe.
Hot (is): Show.
Hot (was): Shaud.
Hour: An-urr.
House: May-zonh.
How?: Cawm-onh?
Hundred: Sonh.
Hung: Pawn.
Hungry: Fanh.
Hunt: Shoss.
Hunted: Shah-say.
Hunter: Shah-surr.
Hurricane: Oh-rah-gonh.
Hurried: Day-pay-shay.
Hurry: Day-pesh.

Hurt: Fay-dee-moll.
Husband: Mah-ree.
I
I: Monh.
Ice: Gloss.
Ice box: Gloss-yair.
Ice cream: Cram.
Icy: Gloss-say: glee-sont.
Idea: Ee-day.
If!: See!
Illegitimate child: Onh-fonh-de-goss.
Illegitimate female: Pew-tanh.
Illegitimate male: Bah-tard.
Imagine: A-modge-in.
Imagined: A-modge-ee-nay.
Imbecile: Am-bay-sill.
Immoral lady: Shyan; pew-tanh.
Important: Am-poe-sibb.
In addition: Oh-see.
In a short time: Tah-lurr.
In a tight spot: Quan-say.
In a while: Donh-anh-a-lonh.
In back of: Onh-nod-yair.
Inch: Poos.
Inebriated: Soo.
Infant: Onh-fonh; bay-bay.
In front of: Dawn-ah-vonh.
In here: Ee-seed-donh.
In hiding: Onh-kah-shett.
Ink: Onk.
In other words: Ah-loss.
Insect: Bay-bet.
Inside: Ont-donh; lot-donh; ee-seed-donh.
Inside out: Ah-lawn-vair.
In some place: Onh-kick-ploss.
Instead of: Pee-toe.
Instigator: Ess-peon-urr.

Insult: Anh-soolt.
Insulted: Anh-sool-tay.
Insurance: An-soo-ronh-suh.
Intercourse: Nick-nick; pee-kay.
In that place: Draught-la.
In the past: Pod-duh-anh-fwaw.
In there: Lot-donh.
Invite: Onh-veet.
Invited: Onh-vee-tay.
In what place: A-You.
Iron: Fair.
Irritated: Chu-rouge.
Island: Ill.
Islet: Ee-let.
It: Say; sah.
Itch: Day-monh-jay.
Itchiness: Day-monh-jay-zonh.
It goes (so-so): Sah-vah.

J

Jalopy: Shah-rett.
Jambalaya: Jhom-buh-lye-ya.
Japanese: Jah-pawn-yea.
Jealous female: Jah-looz.
Jealous male: Jah-loo.
Jellyfish: Blogg.
Job: Jaub.
July: Jweel-yea.
Jump: Sawt.
Jumped: Sow-tay.
June: Jhwanh.
Just: Jhuss.
Just about: Ah-pray-pray; press-kuh.

K

Keep: God.
Kept: God-day.
Kerchief: Tee-yonh.
Key: Clay.

Kick: Anh-cood-pyea.
Kidney: Ronh-yonh.
Kidney stone: Pierre.
Kill: Tu.
Killed: Tway.
Kind (a): Coll-lee-tay.
Kiss: Bross.
Kissed: Onh-bra-say.
Kitchen: Quee-zin.
Knee: Jhnoo.
Kneeling: Dodge-noo.
Knew: Cawn-nu.
Knife: Coo-toe.
Knock: Coinh.
Knocked: Coin-yea.
Knock off from work: Day-bawsh.
Knocked off (from work): Day-bow-shay.
Knot: Neuh.
Know (to): Cawn-nay.
Know (will): Cawn-net; sah-war.
L
Lad: Tee-boog.
Ladder: A-shell.
Lady: Fawm.
Lake: Lock.
Lame: Flee-jay; ess-throw-pyea.
Lamp: Lomp.
Land (a piece of): Tair.
Last (to): Durr.
Last (to be): Dan-yea.
Lasted: Due-ray.
Last month: Mwaw-pah-say.
Last night: Yair-oh-swarr.
Last one: Dan-yair.
Last week: Sman-pah-say.
Last year: Awn-nay-pah-say.
Laugh: Ree.

Laughing: Rear.
Lawn: Coor.
Law: Loll-waw.
Lawyer: Ah-voe-kah.
Laziness: Pah-ress.
Lazy female: Pah-ray-suzz.
Lazy-male: Pah-ray-suh.
Lead: Plonh.
Leak: Cool.
Leaked: Coo-lay.
Lean (to): Pawn-suh.
Lean (to be): Meg; manse.
Leaned: Pawn-shay.
Leaned against: Co-lay; fraught.
Leave: Kit; parr.
Left (side): Barr-ah-gawsh.
Left (went away): Pot-tee.
Left behind: Kee-tay.
Leftover: Rhess; race-tay.
Leg: Jhom.
Lemon: Lee-monh.
Lemonade: Lee-monh-nodd.
Lend: Onh-pray-tay.
Lent (the period before Easter): Kah-ram.
Less: Mwanh.
Let: Kit; less.
Let go: Lawsh.
Let go (did): La-shay.
Letter: Let.
Lettuce: Lat-tu.
Level (a carpenter's tool): Ee-voe.
Level (to be even): A-goll.
Liar: Fay-zurr-duh-mawn-three; mawn-turr.
License: Lee-sawnce.
Lick: Lish.
Licked: Lee-shay.
Lie (a): Mawn-three.

Lie (to): Monh-tuh.
Lie down to sleep: Coosh.
Life: Vee.
Light (a): Leem-yair.
Light (to): Ah-lume.
Light (weight): Lay-jay.
Light bulb: Glaub.
Lightened (become clear): A-clair-see.
Lightning: A-clair.
Like (to): Am.
Like (to be): Cawm.
Limit: Lee-mitt.
Line: Ling.
Linoleum: Tah-pee.
Lion: Lee-onh.
Lips: Lev.
Liquor: Bwaw-sonh; co-loy.
Listen: A-coot.
Listened: A-coo-tay.
Lit: Ah-lume-may.
Little: Pee-tee.
Little aunt: Tee-taunt.
Little female: Teet.
Little male: Tee.
Liver (the): Fwaw.
Lizard: Leez-odd.
Lone: Sull.
Lonesome: On-wee-yont.
Lonesome (was): On-wee-yea.
Long: Lonh.
Long ago: Lonh-tonh-pah-say.
Long time: Lonh-tonh.
Look: God; udd-god.
Looked (at): God-day.
Looked (for): Udd-god-day; shah-say.
Looking: Udd-god-day.
Loose (to get): A-shop.

Loose (got): A-shop-a.
Lose: Pad.
Lost (to have): Foo-tu.
Lost: Pad-du.
Louisiana: La-lose-yan.
Love: Ah-more.
Low: Bah.
Lower (to): Bess.
Lowered: Bay-say.
Low-priced: Bawn-mar-shay.
Lucky: Shawn-suh.
Lure (fishing term): Ah-pah.

M

Macaroni: Mock-ah-roan-nee.
Machine: Ma-shin.
Mad: Fah-shay; shawk.
Madam & Ms: Mah-dom.
Made mad: Show-kay.
Magazine: Mah-gah-zin.
Magnificent: Mag-nee-fick; moan-ee-fick.
Mail: Moll.
Make believe: Fay-ah-crawr.
Make mad: Shawk; show-kay.
Making faces: Free-moose.
Malady: Moll-ah-dee.
Male: Moll.
Male dog: Shyanh.
Malice: Mah-liss; kah-priss.
Malicious: Mah-lease-yeuh.
Mallard (duck): Kah-narr-fronh-say.
Man: Ohm.
Mange: Goll.
Many: Cawn-tee-tay; pleuz-yurr.
Many (too): Dud-throw.
Marble: Con-nick.
March (a month): Mahrse.
Marched: Mar-shay.

Mardi Gras: Mod-dee-grah.
Mark (a): Mock.
Married: Mahr-yea.
Marry: Mah-ree.
Marsh: Mahr.
Marsh gas: Fee-foe-lay.
Mask: Mah; mosque.
Mass (church function): Mess.
Massacre: Mah-sock.
Massacred: Mah-sock-cray.
Mast: Mah.
Match (a): Ah-leem-met.
Material: A-toff.
Mattress: Mott-la.
May (a month): May.
Maybe: Pay-tet.
Maypops: God-nod; grah-nod.
Me: Monh.
Mean female: Moe-vezz.
Mean male: Moe-vay.
Mean person: Hahr-ya.
Mean spirit: Moe-vay-ess-pree.
Measles: La-roo-jawl.
Meat: Vyawn.
Medal: May-die.
Medicine: Mitt-sin.
Meet: Ronh-cont.
Melt: Fawn.
Melted: Fawn-du.
Merited: May-ree-tay.
Mess up: Buh-ree-nay.
Messy: Zee-rob.
Messy female: Sah-laup.
Messy male: Ko-shonh.
Met: Roan-cone-tray.
Middle: Meel-yuh.
Midnight: Man-we.

Mile: Mill.
Milk: Lay.
Milk sack (a fish): Sock-ah-lay.
Million: Meel-yawn.
Mind (the): Sair-vell.
Mind (to): Swainh.
Minded: Swanh-yea.
Mine: Myan; la-myan.
Mink: Blett.
Minor: Mee-nurr.
Minus: Mwanh.
Minute (a): Anh-mee-nuht.
Miracle: Mee-rock.
Mirror: Meer-war.
Mischievous: Ha-yee-sob.
Miserable: Me-zee-rob.
Miserly: Shiss.
Miss (to): Monk.
Missed: Monh-kay.
Mississippi: Me-suh-see-pee.
Mister: Meese-yeuh.
Misunderstood: Moll-cawm-pree.
Mix: Mell.
Mixed: May-lay.
Mockery: Mah-cock-cree.
Mold: Vair-duh-gree.
Monday: Lan-dee.
Money: Arr-jonh.
Monkey: Mah-cock.
Monkeyshines: Mock-ah-cree.
Month: Mwaw.
Moon: Lune.
Moral: Jhuss.
More: Pleuss.
Morning: Ah-vonh-mee-dee; mah-tanh.
Mosquito: Mod-ah-gwanh; moose-tick.
Moss: Moose.

Mother: Mare.
Motor: Mah-shin.
Motor oil: Wrill-duh-see-lan.
Mouse: Soo-ree.
Mouth: Boosh; jull.
Move: Grooi; grew-yuh.
Move (change residences): Day-low-jay.
Moved: Grew-yea.
Much (too): Dud-throw.
Mud: Boo.
Mud diver (a duck): Plawn-jonh.
Mud hole: Trood-boo.
Mule: Mu-lay.
Mumps: La-jaub.
Mushroom: Shop-ee-yawn.
Music: Mu-zick.
Must: Foe-rah.
Mustache: Moose-tosh.
Mustard: Moo-tard.
Mute: Mwet.
Myself: Monh.
N
Nail (a): Clue.
Nail (to): Top-oh-shay.
Nailed: Ah-tosh-shay.
Naked: Nu.
Name: Nonh.
Nanny: Mah-ran; nuh-nan.
Nap: Sawm.
Narrow: A-traught.
Narrow canal for trappers: Thran-noss.
Nausea: Zear.
Nauseous: Moll-oh-curr.
Navel: Nawm-bree.
Near: Pray.
Nearly: Press-kuh; prawsh; ah-pray-pray.
Necessary: Nay-say-sair.

Neck: Coo.
Necklace: Cole-yea.
Necktie: Krah-vott.
Need: Buzz-wanh.
Needle: Igg-weii.
Neighbor: Wuzz-anh.
Neighborhood: Caught.
Neither: Knee.
Nerve: Naff.
Nerve (to have): Too-pay.
Nervous: Nair-vuh.
Nest: Nick.
Never: Jhom-may.
New (is): Noo-voe.
New (was): Nuff.
News: Noo-vell.
Newspaper: Gah-zett; pop-yea.
Next day: Deux-manh.
Next month: Mwaw-pro-shan.
Next one: Pro-shan.
Next week: Sman-pro-shan.
Next year: Awn-nay-pro-shan.
Nickel: San-soo.
Niece: Nyess.
Night: Nwee; swarr.
Night time visit: Vay-yea.
Nine: Nuff.
Nineteen: Deez-nuff.
Ninety: Cot-ruh-vanh-diss.
Nipple: Sues-ronh.
No: Nonh!
No good: Moo-dee; pah-bawn.
Noise: Say-die; shah-rod.
Noisy: Say-die-yuzz.
Noon: Mee-dee.
North: Nor.
Norther: Cood-nor.

Nose: Nay.
Not: Pah.
Not at all: Pah-dee-too.
Not good: Pah-cot-oh-lick; pah-bonh.
Not-here: Pah-ee-see.
Nothing: Odd-yanh.
Nothing at all: Pah-dee-too.
Not over there: Pah-la-bah.
Not straight: Crawsh.
Not together: Pah-onh-sawm.
November: No-vawm.
Novice: Ah-prawn-tee.
Now: Ah-stir.
Nude: Nu.
Numb: Onh-goad-dee.
Number: Loom-er-oh.
Nut (for a bolt): Nwaw.

O

Oak tree: Shan.
Obligated: Oh-blee-gay.
Observed: Ob-sair-vay.
Occupied: Oak-you-pay.
October: Oak-taub.
Odor: Low-durr.
Off: Pah-duh-sue.
Offer: Oh-fair.
Office: Oh-fiss.
Officer: Oh-feece-yea.
Often: Sue-vaunt; fray-conht.
"Oh you poor thing:" Pauve-bet.
Oil: Wrill-duh-see-lan.
Okra: Ghom-bow.
Old man: Vieu; vieu-yuh.
Old woman: Vyeii; Vyea-yuh.
Olive: Oh-liv.
On: Duh-soo.
On board: Ah-bar.

Once: Pod-duh-an-fwaw.
One: An.
One apiece: Pyess; shock.
One time: Anh-fwaw.
Onion: Onh-yonh.
On purpose: Ess-pray.
Only: Sull.
On shore: Ah-tair.
On the feet: Duh-boot.
On the floor: Pot-tair.
On the knees: Dodge-new.
On the lam: Ah-lah-coose.
On the side: Ah-co-tay.
On the sly: Onh-kah-shett.
On top: Onh-lair.
Open (to): Roove.
Open (will): Roo-vair.
Opened: Roo-vairt.
Opening (an): Roo-vair-tour.
Operating: Oh-pay-ray.
Oppose: Ah-pause.
Opposite: Ah-poe-zay.
Orange: Oh-ronge.
Ordinary: Cawm-unh.
Or else: Ought-ruh-monh.
Other one (the): Lawt.
Others: Lays-ought.
Otherwise: Ought-ruh-monh.
Our: Naught.
Outside: Ont-day-your.
Oven: Bah-sin.
Overly foolish: Kah-zock.
Over there: La-bah.
Overturn: Cop-oh-tay.
Owl: Ee-boo.
Oyster: Witt.
Oysters: Daze-zwitt.

P

Pack: Pock-kay.
Paddle: Pah-guy.
Padlock: Cod-nah.
Page: Podge.
Paid: Pay-yea.
Paint: Pan-tour.
Paint brush: Pan-sow.
Painted: Pan-tour-ray.
Painting (a): Port-tray.
Pale: Poll; kah-goo.
Pants: Pot-ah-lonh.
Pap (flour pudding): Boo-yee.
Paper: Pop-yea.
Parade: Pah-rod.
Pardon: Par-donh.
Pardoning: Par-donh-nay.
Parents: Pah-ronh.
Part: More-so.
Particular: Pot-tee-cool-yea.
Partner: Ah-mee; pod-nah.
Part of: Anh-pott-tee.
Pass: Poss; coup.
Passed: Pah-say.
Pass out: Avon-we.
Passed out: A-von-weer.
Past: Pah-say.
Patch (a trawl): Foe-fee-lay; my-yea.
Pay (to): Pay-yuh.
Paying: Pay-yea.
Peach: Pesh.
Pealed: Sonh-nay.
Peanuts: Peace-tosh.
Pear: Pwarr.
Peas: Fev.
Pebble: Kai-you.
Pecan: Pock-on.

Pecan tree: Pock-on-yea.
Peeled: A-pleu-shay.
Peelings: A-kahl; a-pleush.
Pelican: Pee-lee-conh.
Pen (for animals): Pock.
Penance: Pee-nee-tonh-suh.
Pencil: Cray-yonh.
Penny: Anh-soo.
People: Mawn.
Perch (a fish): Pah-tah-sah.
Pepper (black): Pwauve.
Per: Shock.
Perfume: Lay-sawnce.
Perhaps: Pay-tet.
Permission: Pare-me-syonh.
Permit: Pear-me.
Persimmon: Plock-men.
Person: Pear-sawn.
Pester: Onh-bet.
Pestered: Onh-bay-tay.
Photograph: Port-tray.
Physician: Doak-tour.
Pick (to): Pee-kay.
Picked up: Roam-ah-say.
Picker: Peek-urr.
Picket (a): Poe-toe; pee-kay.
Pick for trouble: Pee-co-shay.
Pick through (shrimping term): Three-yea.
Picky: Day-fay-sill.
Picture: Port-tray.
Pie: Tot.
Piece: More-so.
Piece of land: Tair.
Pierce: Pair-say.
Pig (female): Ko-shawn.
Pig (male): Ko shonh.
Pigeon: Pee-jonh.

Pig pen: Pock-ah-ko-shonh.
Pill: Pee-nuel.
Pillow: Oar-yea.
Pin: A-pang.
Pincer: Panse.
Pinch (to): Quanse; panse.
Pinched: Quan-say; pan-say.
Pink: Rawz.
Pipe (for conducting fluids or gas): Tee-yoe.
Pipe (for smoking): Pip.
Pirogue: Pee-raug.
Pistol: Peace-toe-lay.
Pitiful: Thriss.
Place: Ploss.
Plain: Cawm-unh.
Plainer (a hand tool): Gah-lair.
Plank: Plawnsh.
Plant: Plawnt.
Planted: Plonh-tay.
Plate: Ah-syett.
Play: Jew.
Played: Jhway.
Playhouse: Cob-awn.
Pleasure: Play-zear.
Plentiful: Ee-nonh-mooi; ee-nonh-moo-yuh.
Plenty: Boo-coo; planh.
Plowing: Rah-boo-lay.
Plug: Plog.
Plugged: Boo-shay.
Plug up: Boosh.
Plunge: Plawnge.
Plunged: Plawn-jay.
Plump: Grah; grow.
Plump female: Grah.
Plump male: Grow.
Pocket: Pawsh.
Pocketbook: Part-mawn-nay.

Point: Pwant.
Pointed: Pwan-tay.
Poison: Pwaw-zonh.
Poisoned: Pwaw-zonh-nay.
Poison ivy: Abb-ah-la-puss.
Pole: Poe-toe.
Police: Loll waw.
Policeman: Oh-feece-yea.
Polite: Poe-lee.
Pond: Mahr.
Poor: Pauve.
Pop-corn: Tock-tock.
Porch: God-lee.
Porpoise: Marce-wanh.
Post: Poe-toe.
Posterior: Pay-tard; dair-yair.
Pot (to cook in): Bawm.
Potato: Pah-tot; pome-duh-tair.
Potato (sweet): Pah-tot-deuce.
Poultry: Pool.
Pound (to): Tah-pawsh.
Pound (a weight): Liv.
Pour out: Vee-day.
Pout: Boo-day; gran-shay.
Pouter: Boo-duzz; gran-shurr.
Powder: Pood.
Power: Poo-war.
Prank: Nish.
Prayed: Pree-yea.
Prayer (a): Pree-yair.
Preached: Pray-shay.
Pregnant: Plan.
Press: Pezz; fraught.
Pressed against: Pay-zay; fro-tay.
Pretend: Fay-ah-crawr.
Pretty: Bow; joe-lee.
Pretty female: Vie-yawn.

Pretty male: Vie-yawnt.
Price: Pree.
Priced high: Share.
Priced low: Bawn-mod-shay.
Priest: Prett.
Prison: Pree-zone.
Prisoner: Pree-zone-yea.
Profess: Pro-fay-say.
Professor: Pro-fay-surr.
Profit: Pro-feet.
Profited: Pro-fee-tay.
Promenade: Prawm-nay.
Promenading: Prawm-nod.
Promise: Prawm-meer.
Promised: Prawm-mee.
Propeller: Pah-lett.
Property: Pro-pyea-tay.
Prophesy: Pro-fay-say.
Prostitute: Pu-tanh.
Protected: Pro-teck-tay.
Providing: Dah-barr.
Pudding (cajun style): Boo-yee.
Puffed up: Onh-flay.
Pull: Holl.
Pulled: Ha-lay.
Pulley: Poo-lee.
Pump: Pawmp.
Punish: Pu-nee.
Punished: Pu-near.
Purple: Vyawl.
Push: Poos.
Pushed: Poo-say.
Put (did): Mee.
Put (to): May.
Put (will): Met.
Put away: Roam-ah-say.
Put into action: Onh-gah-jay.

Put on clothes: Ah-be-yea.
Put out (a light or fire): A-tanh.

Q

Quarter: Van-san-soo.
Queasiness: Zee-rob; zear.
Queen: Dawm.
Quick: Vitt.
Quiet: Trawn-kill.
Quilt: Quett.
Quite: Tray.
Quite a few: Cawn-tee-tay.

R

Rabbit: La-panh.
Raccoon: Shah-wee.
Radish: Rah-dee.
Rag: Gay-neii.
Rain (the): Pwee.
Raincoat: Cop-oh-see-day.
Rained: Moo-yea.
Raining: Ah-pray-moo-yea.
Raise: Lev; ell-vay.
Raisin: Raise-anh.
Rake (a): Rah-toe.
Rake (to): Rock-lay.
Ran: Coo-ree.
Rancid: Rawn-sid.
Rare: Rahr.
Rat: Rah.
Rather than: Pee-toe.
Razor: Rozz-war.
Read: Lee.
Reading: Leer.
Ready: Pah-ray.
Real: Vray.
Realize: Ah-pear-sue.
Really: Vray-monh; rell-monh.
Recall: Rah-pell.

Recalled: Rah-play.

Red: Rouge.

Redbug: Bet-rouge.

Red fish: Pwaw-sonh-rouge.

Red head: Tet-rouge.

Refrigerator: Gloss-yair.

Regular: Ray-glay.

Reheat: Ray-show-fay.

Relative: Coos-anh.

Remaining: Ress.

Remember: Rah-pell.

Remembered: Rah-play.

Report: Rah-part.

Reported: Rah-part-tay.

Reporter: Rah-part-turr.

Resembling another: Onh-pan-tour.

Respond: Ray-pawn.

Responded: Ray-pawn-du.

Responding: Ray-pawn.

Responsible: Race-pawn-sob.

Rest (to): Arr-poe-zay.

Restaurant: Ess-toe-rah.

Return (to): Vin-near.

Return (will): Ah-roam-nay.

Returned: Vin-nee.

Ribs: Caught.

Rice: Ree.

Rich: Rish.

Rickety thing: Onh-grew-shod.

Rifle: Few-zee.

Rigging on a shrimp boat: Gray-yuh-monh.

Right: Co-reck.

Right (to the): Bar-ah-draught.

Right away: Toot-sweet.

Right in this place: Ee-see.

Right there: Draught la.

Ring (for the finger): Bog.

Rip: Day-shear.
Ripped: Day-she-ray.
River: Reev-yair.
Roach: Rah-vair.
Rob: Vall.
Robbed: Voe-lay.
Rocking chair: Bare-suzz.
Roll (to): Rawl.
Rolled: Roo-lay.
Roller: Roo-low.
Room: Shawm.
Roots: Rah-sin.
Rope: Caud.
Rosary: Shop-play.
Rose (a color): Rawze.
Rotten: Poo-ree.
Round: Ronh.
Rub: Fraught.
Rubbed: Fro-tay.
Rubber (condom): Cop-ought.
Rubber sheet: Pee-sue.
Ruckus: Shah-rod.
Rudder: Goo-vair-nye.
Running: Coo-ree.
Rust: Roo-yuh.
Rusty: Roo-yea.

S

Sabine Indian: Sah-bin; sob (however, this term is derogatory).
Sack: Sock.
Sacred: Bee-nee.
Safe (Cajun style): Gar-mawn-jay.
Said: Deer.
Saint: Sont.
Salad: Sah-lodd.
Salary: Sah-lair.
Salt: Sell.
Salty: Sah-lay.

Same (the): Mam.
Same likeness: Onh-pan-tour.
Same thing: Mam-shawz.
Sand fly: Frop-dah-barr.
Sane: Bawn-ess-pree.
Sang: Shawn-tay.
Sank: Coll-lay.
Santa Clause: La-crish-ten.
Sassafras leaves: Fee-lay.
Satisfy: Sah-teece-fay.
Saturday: Sawm-dee.
Sauce piquant: Sauce-pee-cawnt.
Saucer: Soo-coup.
Sausage: Sow-siss.
Sausage (Cajun style): Boo-danh.
Savage: Sow-vodge.
Save: Sauve.
Saved: So-vay.
Saw (past tense of see): Vue.
Saw (a tool): Syea.
Say: Dee.
Scald: A-show-day.
Scandal: Ess-cawn-dahl.
Scare: Fay-purr.
Scared: Purr.
Scatter: A-pie-yea.
School: A-call.
School teacher: May-tress-day-call.
Schooner: Gwaw-let.
Scissors: See-zoe.
Scrape: A-core-shay.
Scratch: Grott.
Scratched: Grah-fee-yea; grott-tay.
Scratching: Ah-pray-grah-tay.
Screw (a): Ah-viss.
Screw (to): Viss.
Screw driver: Tour-nah-viss.

Screwed: Vee-say.

Sea: Mare.

Sea (at): Ah-la-mare.

Seagull: Gwaw-lonh.

Searched: Share-shay; shoss-say.

Sea sickness: Moll-duh-mare.

Sea-snail: Bee-god-noo.

Season (a): Say-zonh.

Sea turtle: Kah-wan.

Second (a): Anh-duze-yam.

See (to): Waw.

See (will): War.

Seine: Throm-my.

Seemingly: Cawm.

Seems like: Onh-dee-ray; sawm.

Seen: Vue.

Seldom: Rarh-uh.

Sell: Vawn.

Send: Onh-voy.

Sense: Sawnt; ess-pree.

Sensed: Sawn-tay.

Sent: Onh-voy-yea.

Separate: Pah-onh-sawm.

Separate the shrimp from the fish and crabs: Three-yea.

September: Sept-tawm.

Serve (to): Sair.

Served: Sair-vee.

Set free: La-shay.

Set in order: Ah-rawn-jay.

Settle up (fishing term to denote shares): Ray-glay.

Seven: Set.

Seventy: Swaw-sont-diss.

Seventy five: Swaw-sont-cans.

Seventy five cents: Seize-ess-coll-anh.

Several: Pleuz-yurr.

Sew: Cood.

Shack: Cob-awn.

Shake: Sue-coo; throm-blay.

Shaking: Sue-quay; throm-blay.

Shallow: Plot.

Shame: Pee-chay.

Shark: Ray-canh.

Shave: Rozz.

Shaved: Rozz-zay.

She: Ell.

Sheep: Moo-tonh.

Sheepshead (a salt water fish): Koss-bore-go.

Sheet (linen): Drah.

Shells (ammo): Cot-toosh.

Shells (oyster or clam): Grah-vwaw; coke-ee-yuh.

Shells (seafood leftovers): Daze-a-coll.

Sheriff: Shay-riff; loll-waw.

Shined: Bree-yea.

Shiny: Bree-yont.

Ship: Nah-veer.

Shirt: Schmizz.

Shoes: Soo-yea.

Shone: Bree-yea.

Shook: Soo-quay; throm-blay.

Shoot: Tear.

Short: Coort.

Short, curly hair: Boo-klett; free-zett.

Shot: Tee-ray.

Shotgun: Few-zee.

Shoulder: A-paul.

Shout: Creii.

Shouted: Cree-yea.

Shovel: Pell.

Show (to): Monh-tuh.

Showed: Monh-tray.

Shown: Monh-tray.

Shrank: Rop-tee-say.

Shrimp: Shave-rett.

Shrink: Rop-tiss.

Shut-up: Tay-twaw.

Sick (to be): Mah-lodd.

Sickness: Moll-ah-dee.

Side (the): Bar; co-tay.

Sideboard (Cajun style): Gar-monh-jay.

Sidewalk: Bonh-kett.

Sign: Sin.

Signal: Seen-yal.

Signed: Seen-yea.

Sign of the cross: Sin-dah-craw.

Silent: Thrawn-kill.

Silly: Bet.

Silly female: Coo-yawn.

Silly male: Coo-yonh.

Silly person: Zaup; zwaw.

Silver eel (fish): Sob.

Simple: Samp; a-zay.

Sin: Pay-shay.

Since: Day-pue.

Sing: Shawnt.

Singing: Shawn-tay.

Single: Sull.

Sink (to): Coll.

Sinner: Pay-shurr.

Sister: Surr.

Sister-in-law: Bell-surr.

Sit: See.

Sitting: Sear.

Six: Cease.

Sixteen: Says.

Sixty: Swaw-sont.

Skin (the): Poe.

Skin (to): A-core-shay.

Skinny: Manse; meg.

Sky: See-yell.

Slap: Coll-ought; cood-top.

Slapped: Kah-low-tay.

Sleep: Darr.
Sleeping: Door-mere.
Sleepy: Onh-darr.
Slept: Door-me.
Slick: Kah-nye.
Slick surface: Glee-sont.
Slip: Gliss.
Slipped: Glee-say.
Slippery: Glee-sont.
Slop jar: Pah-chawm.
Sloppy: Moll-ah-jawn-tray.
Slow: Deuce-monh.
Slowpoke: Crobb.
Small: Pee-tee.
Small amount: Goot.
Smaller (to get): Rop-tiss.
Smaller (got): Rop-tee-say.
Small (one-layer cake): Gah-lett.
Small speck: Gree-yoe.
Small taste: Goot.
Small town: Vee-lodge.
Small trawl: Trine-ett.
Smart: Smott.
Smart alec: Fawn-chock.
Smash: A-crozz.
Smashed: A-crozz-zay.
Smeared: Buh-ree-nay.
Smell (an unpleasant): Low-durr.
Smell (to): Sonh-tay.
Smell bad: Pway.
Smoke: Boo-cawn.
Smoke cigarettes: Feum.
Smoked: Boo-conh-nay.
Smoked cigarettes: Feum-may.
Smother: A-toof.
Smothered: A-too-fay.
Snake: Sair-pont.

Sneaky female: Mah-lan.
Sneaky male: Mah-lanh.
Sneeze: A-tair-nay.
Snob: Lev-nay.
Snore: Roan-flay.
So: A-banh.
Soap: Sah-vonh.
Socks for females: Show-set.
Socks for males: Show-sonh.
Soda: So-dah; pawp.
Sofa: So-fah.
Soft: Moo.
Soft drink: So-dah.
Soft shelled crabs: Crobb-mall.
Soil (the): Tair.
Soil (to): Sah-lay.
Soiled: Sah-lee.
Soiling: Sah-leer.
Soldier: Soul-dah.
Solemn: So-lem.
Solid: So-lid.
Some: Day.
Some excitement: Dee-shwaw.
Someone: Kay-can.
Someone else: Kay-canned-ought.
Somersault: Kuhl-buht; tumble set.
Something: Kick-shawz; duh-qwaw.
Something else: Kick-shawz-dawt; an-ought-shawz.
Sometimes: Day-fwaw.
Somewhere: Onh-kick-ploss.
Son: Gar-sonh.
Song: Shawn-sonh.
Sore (a): Bow-bow.
Sore (to be): Oh-viff.
Sorrow: La-pan.
Sort: Kah-lee-tay.
Sounded: Sonh-nay.

Sour: Heg.

Soured: Heg-gree.

Sow (a pig; female): Co-shawn.

Spaghetti: Mock-ah-roan-nee.

Speak bad about: May-pree-zay.

Speck: Gree-yoe.

Speckled trout (fish): Thritt.

Spectacles: Lee-net.

Speed: Vah-vitt.

Speedy: Vitt.

Spend: Day-pawn-suh.

Spent: Day-pawn-say.

Spicy: Pee-cawnt.

Spider: Nan-yea.

Spider web: Filled-nan-yea.

Spigot: Roe-bee-nay.

Spirit: Ess-pree; fee-foe-lay.

Spit: Crosh-ah.

Spit (did): Crosh-say.

Spit (to): Crosh.

Spiteful: Ha-ruh-ya.

Splice: Rah-boo-lay.

Splinter: Peek-urr; peek-onh.

Spoiled: Gah-tay.

Spoon: Keel-yair.

Spread about: A-pie-yea.

Spring (a season): Luh-pran-tonh.

Squall: Oh-rodge; granh; tonh-pet.

Square (carpenter's tool): A-cair.

Square (to be): Cod-a.

Squash: A-fyall.

Squashed: A-fyall-lay.

Squeeze: Quanse.

Squeezed: Quan-say.

Squid: Coll-ah-mah.

Squirrel: Nay-cood-uh-yuh.

Stairs: Ess-coll-yea.

Standing: Duh-boot.
Star: A-twall.
Start: Cawn-onh-suh.
Started: Cawm-onh-say.
State: A-tah.
Stay: Ress.
Steal: Vall.
Steel: Fair.
Steer: Goo-vair-nye.
Steps: Ess-coll-yea.
Stew: Freak-ah-say.
Stick (a): Bah-tonh.
Stick (to): Call; pee-kay.
Stiff: Red.
Still: Too-jour; surr-monh.
Still (to be): Trawn-kill.
Stingy: Shiss.
Stink (a): Low-durr.
Stink (to): Pue.
Stir: Bross.
Stirred: Bross-say.
Stole: Voe-lay.
Stomach: Ess-tonh-ah; vaunt.
Stomach ache: Moll-oh-vaunt.
Stone (kidney): Pierre.
Stop: Ah-rett.
Stopped: Ah-ray-tay.
Stopped up: Boo-shay.
Stopper: Boosh-onh.
Store (a): Mogg-ah-zanh.
Storm: Oh-rah-gonh.
Story teller: Rah-cawn-turr.
Straight: Draught.
Strange: Drawl.
Stranger: A-throng-jay.
Strangle: A-throng-glay.
Strike (to): Fly-yea.

String: Fee-sell; fill.
Strong: Far.
Stuck to: Pree.
Stuck (to be): Onh-fawn-say.
Stuck up: Lev-nay; craw.
Study: A-tood-yea.
Stuffed: Boo-shay.
Stuffiness: Shah-lurr.
Stump: Schoose.
Stunk: Pway.
Stupid person: Am-bay-sill; goof-onh; zaup.
Succeed: Rue-see.
Suck: Suss.
Sucked: Sue-say; tay-tay.
Suffer: Pah-tee.
Suffered: Pah-tear.
Suffocate: A-toof.
Suffocated: A-too-fay.
Sugar: Sook.
Suitcase: Vah-liss.
Summer: A-tay.
Sunday: Dee-monh-shuh.
Supper: Soo-pay.
Suppose: Say-poe-zay.
Surprise: Surr-pree.
Surrounding: Tool-tour.
Swallow: Onh-voll.
Swallowed: Onh-voll-lay.
Swamp: Sip-pree-yair.
Sweat: Sway.
Sweating: Ah-pray sway.
Sweep: Boll-yea.
Sweet: Do.
Swell-up: Onh-flay.
Swim: Nah-jay.
Swing: Gah-lawn-suh.
Swinging: Gah-lawn-say.

Swollen: Oh-viff; onh-flay.

Swung: Gah-lawn-say.

System: Cease-tawm.

T

Table: Tobb.

Tablet (to write in): Tobb-let.

Tail: Chuh.

Tailbone: Croup-yonh.

Take: Pronh.

Take a break: Arr-poe-zay.

Take down: Ah-bott.

Taken: Pree.

Take: Pronh.

Talk: Poll.

Talked: Poll-lay.

Tangle (to): Mel.

Tangled: May-lay.

Taste (a): Goot.

Taste (to): Goo.

Tasted: Goo-tay.

Tattle: Rah-pawt.

Tattled: Rah-pawt-tay.

Tattler: Rah-pawt-turr.

Tax: Tox.

Tea: Tay.

Teacher: May-thress.

Tear (to): Day-shear.

Tears: Lay-lamb.

Teeth: Donh.

Tell: Dee.

Tell (will): Deer; rah-cawn-tay.

Tell a big lie: Vawn-turr.

Tell a small lie: Mawnt.

Temper: Co-lair.

Temper tantrum: Crizz.

Tempest: Tonh-pet.

Temporary patch a trawl: Foe-fee-lay.

Ten: Dee; diss.

Ten cents: Dee-soo.

Tender: Tawn.

Tend to: Swanh-yuh.

Tended to: Swanh-yea.

Terrible: Tay-rib.

Terrific: Monh-knee-fick.

Thanks: Mare-see.

That: Sah!

The (singular): La.

The (plural): Lay.

Them: Uzz-ought.

The one following: Pro-shan.

The others: Lays-ought.

There: La.

Thermometer: Tair-monh-met.

The side of: Bar.

They: Uzz-ought.

Thick: A-pay.

Thigh: Quiss.

Thin: Manse; meg.

Thing: Ah-fair; shawz.

Think: Craw; jong; pawnse.

Thirsty: Swaff.

Thirteen: Threzz.

Thirty: Thront.

Thistle: Shod-ronh.

Those: Lays-ought.

Thought: Ee-day; jong-glay; pawn-say.

Thousand (a): Anh-mill.

Three: Thraw.

Threw: God-oh-shay.

Threw up: Vaum-me.

Throat: Gaudge.

Throbbed: Lawn-say.

Throw: Gah-rawsh.

Throw a fit: Crizz.

Throwing: Ah-pray-god-oh-shay.
Throw-up: Day-gull-lay; vonh-me.
Thumb: Poos.
Thunder: Tawn-air.
Thursday: Jhuh-dee.
Ticket: Tee-kett.
Tickle: Shot-too-yuh.
Tickled: Shot-too-yea.
Ticklish: Shot-too-yuzz.
Tide: Mah-ray.
Tie (a): Krah-vott.
Tie (to): Onh-mod.
Tied: Onh-mod-a.
Tiger: Teeg.
Tight: Say-ray.
Tighten: Sair.
Tightwad: Shiss.
Time (a): Fwaw; tonh.
Time (the): Urr.
Tin: Zanh.
Tin cup: Pant.
Tire (a): Bawn.
Tire (to): Fah-tick.
Tired: Fah-tee-kay; a-she-nay.
Tiresome: Fah-tee-cont.
Tobacco: Tah-bah.
To be rid of: Day-fair.
Today: Ah-jourd-wee.
Toe: Oat-aye.
Together: Onh-sawm.
To have lost: Foo-tu.
Toilet: Ko-maud.
Toilet paper: Pop-yade-torsh.
Told: Dee; rah-cawn-tay.
Told a big lie: Vonh-tay.
Tolled: Sonh-nay.
Tomato: Tawm-ott.

Tomorrow: Deuh-manh.

Tomorrow night: Deuh-manh-oh-swarr.

Tongue: Long.

Tonight: Ah-swarr.

Tonsils: Oll-wet.

Too: Oh-see.

Took: Pree.

Took out: Oh-tay.

Tool: Oo-tee.

Tools: Zoo-tee.

Too much: Dud-throw.

Tooth: Donh.

Toothache: Moll-oh-donh.

Top: Taup; fay.

Tore: Day-she-ray.

To sort out shrimp from the fish, and crabs caught in a trawl: Three-yea.

To the top: Onh-lair.

Touch: Toosh.

Touched: Too-shay.

Towel: Sair-viet.

Toy: Bay-bell.

Traffic: Trah-fick.

Trap (a): Pyedge.

Trapped: Pyea-jay.

Trapper: Pyedge-urr.

Trash: Dree-guy.

Trawl (a): Thrawl.

Trawl (to): Throw-lay.

Trawling: Ah-pray-throw-lay.

Trawl webbing: Fill.

Treat (someone ill): Thrett.

Treated: Tray-tay.

Treater: Tray-turr.

Treating: Thray-tay.

Tree: Bwaw.

Tremble: Throm.

Trembled: Throm-blay.

Trembling: Free-sonh.

Trick: Nish.

Tricked: Coo-yonh-nay.

Trickle: Pee-say.

Tricky: Kah-nye.

Tricky (female): Mah-lan.

Tricky (male): Mah-lanh.

Tried: Ah-say-yea.

Trouble: Meez-air; throob; throck-ah.

Troubled: Throck-ah-say.

Troubles: Throck-ah.

Trouser: Pot-ah-lonh.

Trouser zipper: Bra-get.

Trout: Thritt.

Trout (green): Thritt-vair.

True: Vray.

Truth: Vay-ree-tay.

Truthful: Awn-net.

Try: Ah-say-yea.

Try-net: A small trawl pulled behind a shrimp boat.

Tub: Bye.

Tuesday: Mod-dee.

Turn (a): Tour; vee-ray.

Turn (to): Veer.

Turned: Tour-nay; vee-ray.

Turned end for end: Vee-rayed-boot.

Turn over: Cop-ought.

Turned over: Cop-oh-tay.

Turtle: Tore-tu.

Twelve: Dooze.

Twelve noon: Mee-dee.

Twenty: Vanh.

Twenty five: Van-sank.

Twenty five cents: Van-san-soo.

Two: Deuh.

Type (a): Coll-ee-tay.

U

Ugly female: Vee-lan.
Ugly male: Vee-lanh.
Ulcer: Ool-sair.
Umbrella: Pah-rah-sall.
Unable to speak: Myett.
Uncle: Nonk.
Unclean: Sahl.
Under: Ont-sue.
Under aged: Mee-nurr.
Under shirt: Schmizz-daunt-sue.
Understand: Conh-prawn.
Understood: Conh-pree.
Underwear: Cawn-sonh.
Undo: Day-fay.
Undoing: Day-fair.
Undomesticated: Mah-roan.
Unhook: Day-crawsh.
Unlight: A-tanh.
Unlit: A-tan.
Unsavory: Zee-rob.
Unscrew: Day-viss.
Unscrewed: Day-vee-say.
Up: Onh-lair.
Up the bayou: Onh-hoe.
Urge: Onh-vee.
Urinate: Pee-say.
Us: Knees-ought.
Use (to): Uzz.
Used: You-zay.
U-shaped nail: Cromp.

V

Vacation: Vah-cawn-suh.
Valise: Vah-liss.
Value: Vah-lurr.
Varnish: Vair-nee.
Verity: Vay-ree-tay.

Very: Tray.
Very good: Mawn-ee-fick.
Village: Vee-lodge.
Vinegar: Vee-neg.
Violet: Vyoe-lay.
Viper: Vee-pair.
Visit: Prawm-nay.
Visited: Vee-zee-tay; row-die-yea.
Visitors: Cawm-pawn-yee.
Voice: Vwaw.
Vomit: Day-gull-lay; vonh-meer.
Vote: Vaught.
Voted: Voe-tay.

W

Wait: Ess-pair.
Waited: Ess-pay-ray.
Wake (a): Vay-yea.
Walk: Mosh.
Walked: Mosh-shay.
Wall: Awn-too-rodge.
Wallet: Pawt-mawn-nay.
Wanted: Voo-lay.
War: Gair.
Warmer (got): Ray-show-fay.
Warmth: Shah-lurr.
Was better: Bawn.
Was drunk: Soo-lay.
Was good: Bonh.
Wash: La-vay.
Wash board: Froat-war.
Wash-cloth: Sair-viet.
Washing powder: Pood-ah-la-vay.
Wash tub: Bye-ah-la-vay.
Wasp: Gep.
Wasp nest: Nick-de-gep.
Waste (to): Goss-pee-yea.
Watch (a): Monh-tuh.

Watch (to): Get.
Watched: Gay-tay; ob-sair-vay.
Watch over: Swanh-yea.
Water: Oh.
Water moccasin (a snake): Cong-oh.
Watery passage: Coop.
Waves: Lay-lawm.
Way: Mawn-yair.
We: Knees-ought.
Wear: Part.
Wedding: Gnaw-suh.
Wednesday: Make-ruh-dee.
Week: Sman.
Weight: Pwaw; pezz.
Weighed: Pay-zay.
Well then: A-banh.
Went: Ah-tay.
Went forward: Ah-vonh-say.
Wet: Thromp.
Wet (was): Throm-pay.
What: Key?
What's left: Ress.
What's that you say: Anh?
What's wrong?: Key-ya?
Wheel: Roo.
Wheelbarrow: Bear-wet.
Where: A-you?
Which one A-kell?
Whiskey: Wees-key.
Whistle: See-flay.
Whittle: Shock-oh-tay.
Whole lot of: Boo-coo.
Whore: Pu-tanh.
Why: Ko-fair?
Wide: Lodge.
Widow: Vuv.
Widower: Vuff.

Wife: Vee-aye-yuh; fawm.
Wild: Mah-roan.
Will: Vah.
Will be: Vah-ett.
Will do: Vah-fair.
Will see: Vah-war.
Wind (the): Vonh.
Window: Shah-see.
Window pane: Vitt.
Windy: Vawn-tay.
Wine: Vanh.
Wings: Zell.
Winter: Ee-vair.
Wiped: Swee-yea.
With: Ah-veck.
Without: Sonh.
Without clothes: Nu.
Without shame: Too-pay.
Without shoes: Nu-pyea.
Woeful: Thriss.
Woke up: Ray-vay-yea.
Woman: Fawm; fee-mell.
Womb: Mair.
Women: Day-fawm; day-fee-mell.
Won: Goin-yea.
Wood: Bwaw.
Wood rat: Rod-bwaw.
Word: Moe; pah-rawl.
Work: Oove-rodge.
Work (to): Trah-vie.
Worked: Trah-vie-yea.
Worm: Vair.
Worn out (tired): A-sheen-nay.
Worried: Throck-ah-say.
Worth: Vah-lurr; voe.
Wound (a): Bow-bow.
Wound (to): Blay-say.

Wrestle: Lu-tay.
Write: Cree.
Written: Cree-yea.
Wrong: Moll.
Wrote: A-cree.

Y

Yard (lawn): Coor.
Yard (three feet): Thraw-pyea; yodd.
Yawn: Bye-yea.
Year: Awn-nay.
Yell: Cree-yea.
Yell (what you scream for a minor hurt): Aye-yie.
Yell (what you scream for a major hurt): Aye-yuh-yie.
Yellow: Jawn.
Yes: Weh.
Yesterday: Yair.
Yet: Too-jour; surr-monh.
You: Twaw; voo.
You all: Yall; wooz-ought.
Young: Jan.
Your: Vaught.
Yours: La-tyan.

Z

Zipper: Bra-gett.

Cajun Surnames

"You've got to be kidding me son" said the Captain, with the two silver bars on his collar gleaming in the yellow sun. "How in the world do you get 'Roby-show' out of Robichaux? It looks more like 'Rob-ick-hawks.'" "Well" my friend say back at him, "Dat's de only way we know how to say it sir."

Maybe the Captain had a point there, but I'm sure that he's not alone. Many of our names don't look like the way we actually say them. However, you dance with the one that brung you. That's how we learned, and believe me, it's not just a simple matter of behavior modification. Cajuns are just plain hard to un-learn. My good friend Chuck Evans probably sums it up best: "You can call me anything that you want to, but just don't call me late for dinner." The following list gives the accurate spelling of some of the most common Cajun surnames, and how they really sound.

Abadie: Abba-dee

Arcement: R-see-mon

Aucoin: Oak-wanh

Autin: Oh-tanh

Badeaux: Bad-oh

Barrios: Barry-yoss

Batiste: Bah-teece

Becnel: Beck-nell

Benoit: Ben-waw

Allemand: Ollie-monh

Arceneaux: R-sun-oh

Authement: Oh-tay-monh

Babineaux: Babbin-oh

Barrilleaux: Barrel-oh

Bascle: Bask-ull

Baudoin: Bode wanh

Belanger: Blawn-jay

Bergeron: Badger-onh

Bienvenue: Be-in-vin-new

Blanchard: Bland-chard

Bonvillain: Bow-vee-lanh

Bordelon: Board-uh-lonh

Boudreaux: Bood-row

Bourg: Berg

Breaux: Bro

Broussard: Brew-sard

Buquet: Bue-kay

Caillouet: Kai-you-wet

Callais: Coll-lay

Carlos: Car-loss

Celestine: Sell-us-tanh

Chabert: Shah-bear

Champagne: Shom-pine

Chatignier: Shot-in-yea

Cheramie: Share-uh-me

Clement: Clay-monh

Collins: Coll-lens

Cromier: Chrome-yea

Cuneo: Coony-oh

Daigle: Day-gull

Dantin: Dawn-tanh

Defelice: Day-fay-lease

Dehart: Dee-heart

Deroche: Day-rawsh

Detillier: Day till-yea

Dion: Dee-yawn

Domangue: Doe-mang

Dubois: Doob-waw

Duplantis: Do-plan-tiss

Duthu: Do-too

Eschete: Esh-tay

Fakier: Fa-kay

Fanguy: Fawn-ghee

Fazzio: Fazzy-yoe

Folse: False

Billiot: Bill-yott

Bollinger: Bah-lynn-jurr

Boquet: Bow-kay

Boudloche: Bood-lawsh

Boudwin: Bode-wanh

Bourgeous: Booj-waw

Brien: Bree-yanh

Brunet: Brew-nay

Cadiere: Cod-yair

Callahan: Collar-hand

Cancienne: Con-see-yanh

Carrere: Kah-rare

Cenac: Sin-ack

Chaisson: Schyess-onh

Charpentier: Sharr-pent-yea

Chauvin: Show-vanh

Chouest: Swesh

Cloutier: Cloat-yea

Comeaux: Comb-oh

Chrochet: Crow-shay

Cunningham: Cun-ing-ham

Danos: Dan-awss

Dardar: Darr-darr

Degruise: Dee-greez

Delahoussaye: Dell-uh-who-say

Derouen: Durr-wanh

Detiveaux: Detty-voe

Disotell: Dezz-oh-tell

Doucet: Do-say

Duet: Do-way

Dupre: Do-pray

Engeron: R-juh-ronh

Fabre: Fobb

Falgout: Foul-goo

Faucheaux: Foe-shay

Fesi: Fee-see

Fonseca: Fawn-see-cah

Fontenot: Found-ten-oh

Foret: Foe-ray

Fournier: Foon-yea

Friloux: Free-lou

Frissella: Fruh-sell-uh

Gaidry: Gade-ray

Galliano: Galley-an-oh

Gaudet: Go-day

Gautreaux: Goat-row

Giroir: Jeer-war

Gisclair: Jiss-clair

Gonsoulin: Gown-suh-lun

Grabert: Grah-bear

Granier: Grand-yea

Gregoire: Greeg-war

Grizaffi: Grizz-ah-fee

Guenoit: Ghee-no

Gueydon: Gay-donh

Guidroz: Geed-rose

Guidry: Gid-ray

Guillot: Gill-yott

Hebert: A-bear

Himel: He-mel

Hutchinson: Hutch-in-son

Jaccuzzo: Juh-cooz-uh

Juneau: Jew-know

Knoblock: No-block

Labat: Luh-bott

Lacoste: Luh-cost

Lafleur: Luh-flurr

Landry: Land-ray

Lajaunie: Luh-journey

Lapeyre: Lop-air

Lapeyrouse: Lap-uh-rues

Larussa: Luh-roo-suh

LeBlanc: Luh-blonh

LeBoeuf: Luh-buff

Lecompte: Luck-ont

Ledet: Luh-day

Legard: Luh-guard

Lirette: Lee-ret

Livas: Live-us

Lodrigue: Load-rig

Lottinger: Lot-in-jurr

Louviere: Loov-yair

Lovell: Love-ull

Luke: Luke

Malbrough: Marl-brew

Marmande: Mar-mawn

Maronge: Muh-ronge

Matherne: Muh-turn

Mayeaux: May-yoe

McElroy: Mackle-roy

Melancon: May-loans-onh

Molaison: Moe-lay-zone

Monnier: Moan-yea

Mouton: Moo-tonh

Naquin: Knock-anh

Olivier: Oh-liv-ee-yea

Ordoyne: R-doin

Ogeron: Or-juh-ronh

Oubre: Oob-ruh

Palmisano: Pal-miss-an-oh

Parfait: Par-fay

Pellegrin: Pelly-granh

Peltier: Pelt-yea

Pertuit: Purr-tweet

Picou: Pee-coo

Pierron: Pyea-ronh

Pinell: Pee-nell

Pitre: Pee-tray

Pizzolatto: Pizz-uh-lot-uh

Plaisance: Play-zonh

Poincot: Pwanh-sonh

Pontiff: Pawn-tiff

Portier: Port-yea

Prestenbach: Press-ton-back

Prevost: Pray-voo

Prosperie: Pross-per-ee

Robichaux: Row-be-show

Rodrigue: Rod-rig

Rosseau: Roo-so

Roussell: Roo-sell

Saia: Sigh-uh

Samanie: Some-uh-knee

Saucier: So-see-yea

Savoie: Sah-vwaw

Schexnayder: Sheck-snide-urr

Sevin: Save-anh

Soigner: Swan-yea

Solet: So-lay

Soudelier: Sue-dell-yea

Stoufflet: Stoof-lay

Tauzin: Toes-anh

Theriot: Terr-yoe

Thibodeaux: Tibb-uh-doe

Tevit: Tee-vay

Toups: Toops

Trahan: Trah-honh

Trosclair: Throws-clair

Usie: You-zay

Verdin: Verd-anh

Verette: Vuh-rett

Voclain: Voke-lanh

Voisin: Wuzz-anh

Waguespack: Wag-us-pack

Yakupsack: Yack-up-sack

Zeringue: Zuh-rang

CRAZY EUPHEMISMS

(How to say you're crazy without saying you're crazy)

His breen's out to lunch.

She's coo-coo.

His scale's a few pounds off.

You nuts.

She's fall.

He's foo-net.

You nuttier dan a fruit cake.

His icebox don't freeze too good.

Her calendar's got a month missing.

He's kah-zock.

You couldn't start a fire with a match.

His clock only got eleven hours on it.

She ain't wrapped too tight.

Gordon J. Voisin

He's almost as smart as a stoopid idiot.

Yoe wheel's got some spokes missing.

Her hotel room ain't got no pass key.

He's ess-throw-yea in the head.

Her allavator stop pretty short of de top floor.

He's got only one oar in de water.

Her IQ is only one point higher dan a dead neutral rat.

I tink her 'lectricity's been turned off.

Yoe motor ain't got no battery.

His breen's on strike against tinking.

She got hit two times twice on de head.

Yoe breen work about as good as an Edsel car.

If day added 50 points to yoe IQ it'll still be under 100.

All of yoe sparkplugs ain't firing.

He left his breen giff-rapped unda' the Christmas tree.

If day put yoe breens in a mosquito it would fly backward.

He ain't playing with no full deck.

Her television's on but she only got a fuzzy picture.

Day don't make no microscope powerful enough to do breen surgery on you.

Her 'lectric box don't got no fuse.

He figure dat two plus two equals nuttin.

Her rady-ater got a leak.

His tawlett don't flush.

Day put a screen door on dare attic.

His front door's at de back of his house.

Her Canadian goose come from Japan.

His flowers don't bloom.

He's got all de regular holes in his head 'cept he got one extra ware his breen leak out.

Yoe frog jump good, 'cept it don't quite reach de lily pad.

His eyeglasses loss a win-duh.

He put a for-sale sign on his mailbox.

His breens got all screwed up by a ball-ping hamma.

She's one penny short of a dolla.'

Anatomy of a Cajun

Ahl-wet: Tonsils.
A-paul: Shoulder.
Awss: Bones.
Boosh: Mouth.
Car: Bowels.
Caught: Ribs.
Croup-yonh: Tailbone.
Curr: Heart.
Dair-yair: Behind.
Doe: Back.
Donh: Teeth.
Dwaw: Finger.
Ess-tome-ah: Stomach.
Fee-gurr: Face.
Fess: Buttocks.
Fonh: Behind.
Fronh: Forehead.
Fwaw: Liver.
Gaudge: Throat.
Geez-yea: Gizzard.
Jhnoo: Knee.
Jhom: Leg.
Jull: Mouth.
Lev: Lips.

Long: Tongue.
Mair: Womb.
Manh: Hand.
Naff: Nerves.
Nawm-bree: Navel.
Oat-aye: Toes.
Poos: Thumb.
Pyea: Foot.
Quiss: Thigh.
Ronh-yonh: Kidney.
Sair-vell: Brain.
Schfeuh: Hair.
Sonh: Blood.
Sue-see: Eyebrows.
Tay-ten: Breasts.
Tet: Head.
Vaunt: Belly.
Zeuh: Eyes.

Nicknames

(People that I know and many I don't know their real names)

Ahl-fair	Ahl-fridd	Aid-war	Anna-yawna
Aunt Doady	Basie	Bee-lay	Big A
Big-boy	Big-head	Big L	Bird Lady
Black-sack	Blawn	Bow-been	Boo-chay
Bree-gonh	Brud	Bummy	Cah-doo
Cawm	Chicky	Chiss	Chocky
Chonh	Chonky	Chross	Chubby
Clee-say	Cless	Clo-fah	Co-co
Con	Cookie	Cooksie	Coo-lonh
Cop-sin	Crack	Dah-dah	Dah-sue
Day-den	Deanie	Dee-dean	Dee-lee-nah
Die-me	Ding	Dock	Doe-ghee
Doffy	Donk	Doo-be	Dookey
Drawz	Dr. Kildare	Duel-vah	Duggy
Duffy	Ee-bee	Ee-rell	Eight ball
Ell-jay	Ell-rell	Flooky	Frog
Fromp	Gay-lonh	Ghinny	Gizzard
Glai-yeez	Goldielocks	Golly-bawt	Got-oh
Grinny	Grow Black	Ha-wee	Hammer
Holy Cow	Jimmy Boy	Jock-um	Joe-bee
Joe-row	Junja Boy	Kah-lock	Kah-yea
Kay-ling	Keet-say	Key	Koss-pah-lett

La-panh	Looky	Lou-la	Lou-lou
Mader-etts	Manny	Mawn-egg	May-may
Me-low	Me-yawn	Miss La-lee	Miss tah-siss
Miss San Tay	Miss Wheel say	Miss wee-nay	Miss Zoo
Mister Dub	Mister Fatty	Mister Goo-lee	Mock-oh
Muncie	Nah-nah	Neek-less	Neeny
Neggie	Nella	Nin	Nonk Ahl-bear
Nonk Black	Nonk Boy	Nonk Chidd	Nonk Coon
Nonk Day	Non Dodd	Nonk Frair	Nonk Lean Zay
Nonk Nall	Nonk Noon	Nonk June	Nonk Tee-ree
Nonk Yawn	Nonk Yoot	Nonk Yoss	Noo-fray
Noonie	Noonie Bell	No Way	Oh-lamp
Onh-twan	Oos-tosh	Ott-tour	Pah-dee-too
Pah-lick	Pay-chonh	Pee-jay	Peeky
Pee-lee	Pee-rot	Pee-yoe	Pod-odd-yanh
Poker	Pony	Pookie	Poul
Prune	Puh-nook	Pyonnie	Quank
Rat	Rawn-kay	San-soo	Shine
Shoe-shoe	Skunk	Smile	Snake
Speedy	Sunny	Tair	Tay-tanh
Tay-tit	Tee Chime	Tee Dog	Tee Don
Tee Joe	Tee Kin	Tee Loney	Tee Lou
Tee Man	Tee Muy	Tee Neg	Tee Nonk Sock
Teet Noon	Tee Toe	Teetsy	Tee Wee
Tee Will	Tee Won	Tezz	Tie-yonh
Tight	Tiny	Too-lou-lou	Too-shay
Too-too	Tootsie	Tore-ya	Tuh-lutt
Tuh-tutt	Tutty	Van sue	Vay-lynn
Wheel-fridd	Wheel-less	Whitey	Winky
Word	Yawn	Yanny	Yawn-knee

COLORS

Bleux: Blue.
Blonh: White.
Gree: Gray.
Jawn: Yellow.
Nwarr: Black.
Oh-ronge: Orange.
Rawz: Pink.
Vyawl: Purple.
Vyoe-lay: Violet.

Insects and Things That Crawl

Bet-rouge: A red bug.
Co-co-dree: A crocodile.
Congo: A water moccasin.
Crop-oh: A frog.
Frawm-mee: Ants.
Khree-kett: Cricket.
Kai-monh: An alligator.
Lees-odd: A lizard.
Nan-yea: A spider.
Puss: A flea.
Rah-vair: A roach.
Sair-pont: A snake.
Vee-pair: A viper.

ANIMALS AND FOUR-LEGGED THINGS

Annie-moe: Cattle; animal.
Buff: A bull.
Cob-ree: A goat.
La-panh: A rabbit.
Lee-onh: Lion.
Mah-cock: A monkey.
Mu-lay: A mule.
Rah: A rat.
Rod-bwaw: A wood rat.
Schfawl: A horse.
Shah: A cat.
Shah-wee: A raccoon.
Shom-oh: A camel.
Shyan: A female dog.
Shyanh: A male dog.
Soo-ree: A mouse.
Vawsh: A cow.

At What Time

Ah-jourd-dwee: Today.
Ah-pray: After.
Ah-prayed-manh: The day after tomorrow.
Ah-pray-mee-dee: The afternoon; after 12 noon.
Ah-stir: Now.
Ah-vonh-mee-dee: The morning; before 12 noon.
Ah-vonh: Before.
An-fwaw: At one time; once.
Anh-dee-mee-yurr: A half an hour.
Anh-duze-yam: A second.
Anh-mee-nuht: A minute.
An-ought-fwaw: Another time.
An-urr: An hour.
A-tay: The summer.
Awn-nay: A year.
Awn-nay-pah-say: Last year.
Awn-nay-pro-shan: Next year.
Bawn-urr: Early.
Dan-yair: The last one.
Donh-anh-a-lonh: In a minute; shortly.
Day-fwaw: Sometimes.
Deuh-manh: Tomorrow.
Deuh-manh-oh-swarr: Tomorrow night.
Ee-vair: The winter.

Jour: The daytime.
June-nay: A day.
Lawn-manh: The next day.
Lawn-tonh-pah-say: A long time ago.
Luh-pran-tonh: The Spring.
Man-wee: Midnight.
Mee-dee: Noon.
Mwaw-pah-say: Last month.
Mwaw-pro-shan: Next month.
Nwee: The nighttime.
Oh-tawm: Autumn.
Prawm-yair: First.
Pro-shan: The next one.
Sman: A week.
Sman-pah-say: Last week.
Sman-pro-shan: Next week.
Swarr: The nighttime.
Tah-lurr: After while; in a minute.
Yair: Yesterday.
Yair-oh-swarr: Last night.

Food, Beverages and Such

Bah-nawn: Banana.
Bay-thrauv: Beets.
Ben: Beans.
Boo-danh: Boudin (Cajun sausage).
Burr: Butter.
Co-cawm: Cucumber.
Coo-bee-yawn: A mild Sauce Piquant, beginning with a roo.
Cram: Cream; ice cream.
Fev: Beans.
Fev-plot: Butter beans.
Frawm-modge: Cheese.
Freak-ah-say: Stew.
Froo: Fruit.
Fwaw: The liver.
Gah-tow: Cake.
Geez-yea: The gizzard.
Ghom-bow: Gumbo.
Johm-buh-lye-ya: Jambalaya.
Kah-fay: Coffee.
Kah-rawt: Carrot.
Lay: Milk.
Lay-tu: Lettuce.
Lee-monh-odd: Lemon aid.
Lye: Garlic.

Mock-ah-rawn-nee: Macaroni.
Moo-tard: Mustard.
Myell: Honey.
My-yee: Corn.
Oh: Water.
Oh-liv: Olive.
Oh-ronge: Orange.
Onh-yonh: Onion.
Pah-tot: Potato.
Pah-tot-dooce: Sweet potato.
Panh: Bread.
Pawm: Apple.
Pawp: Soda pop; cola.
Peace-tosh: Peanut.
Pesh: Peach.
Plock-men: Persimmon.
Pock-awn: Pecan.
Pwarr: Pear.
Pwauve: Pepper.
Rah-dee: Radish.
Ray-zanh: Raisin.
Roo: Flour sauce.
Sauce-pee-cawnt: Sauce Piquant.
Sell: Salt.
Sell-rhee: Celery.
Shock-oh-la: Chocolate.
Sook: Sugar.
Soop: Soup.
Sow-sis: Sausage.
Tawm-ott: Tomato.
Tay: Tea.
Tock-tock: Popcorn.
Tot: Pie.
Uff: Egg.
Vee-neg: Vinegar.
Vyawn: Meat.
Vyawn-moo-lay: Ground meat.

By the Numbers

An: One.
Anh-sonh: One hundred.
Cans: Fifteen.
Cease: Six.
Cot: Four.
Cot-awz: Fourteen.
Cot-ruh-vanh: Eighty.
Cot-ruh-vanh-diss: Ninety.
Deez-nuff: Nineteen.
Deez-set: Seventeen.
Deez-witt: Eighteen.
Deux: Two.
Diss: Ten.
Dooz: Twelve.
Kah-ront: Forty.
Nuff: Nine.
Onz: Eleven.
Sank: Five.
Sank-cont: Fifty.
Says: Sixteen.
Set: Seven.
Swaw-sont: Sixty.
Swaw-sont-diss: Seventy.
Thraw: Three.

Threzz: Thirteen.
Thront: Thirty.
Vanh: Twenty.
Wit: Eight.

Months of the Year

Ah-vreel: April.
Ah-woo: August.
Day-sawm: December.
Fev-ree-yea: February.
Jawn-vyea: January.
Jwanh: June.
Jweel-yea: July.
Mahrse: March.
May: May.
No-vawm: November.
Oak-taub: October.
Sept-tawm: September.

Days of the Week

Dee-mawnsh: Sunday.
Jhuh-dee: Thursday.
Lan-dee: Monday.
Make-ruh-dee: Wednesday.
Mod-dee: Tuesday.
Sawm-dee: Saturday.
Vaunt-ruh-dee: Friday.

SEAFOOD

A-cray-viss: Crawfish.
Awn-ghee: An eel.
Bee-god-noo: A sea snail.
Blogg: Jellyfish.
Coll-ah-mah: Squid.
Conk: A sea snail.
Crobb: Crab.
Crobb-mall: Soft-shelled crab.
Coss-boor-go (fish): A sheepshead.
Muy-nwarr (fish): A black mullet.
Pah-tah-sah (fish): A perch, bream.
Plea (fish): A flounder.
Pwaw-sonh: A fish.
Pwaw-sonh-rouge: A red fish.
Ray-canh: A shark.
Shave-rett: Shrimp.
Sob: A silver eel.
Tawm-bow (fish): A black drum.
Thritt: A trout (speckled, white or green).
Tore-tu: A turtle.
Zwitt: Oysters.

THINGS THAT FLY

Brew-low: A gnat.
Doe-gree: A kind of duck.
Ee-boo: An owl.
Frop-dah-barr: A sand fly.
Gep: Wasp.
Gwaw-lonh: A seagull.
Kah-narr: A duck.
Kah-narr-frawn-say: A French duck; mallard.
Moose-tick: A mosquito.
Moosh: A fly.
Moosh-ah-myell: A honey bee.
Pee-jonh: A pigeon.
Plawn-john: A type of duck.
Pool-doe: A kind of duck.
Poul: A chicken.
Zanh-zanh: A type of duck.
Zwaw: A goose.
Zwaw-zoe: A bird.

RELATIONS

Bell-surr: Sister-in-law.
Bow-frair: Brother-in-law.
Cooz-anh: Cousin.
Frair: Brother.
Groan-mare: Grandmother.
Groan-pair: Grandfather.
Mair: Mother.
Nonk: Uncle.
Nuh-nan: Godmother.
Nyess: Niece.
Pah-ranh: Godfather.
Pair: Father.
Surr: Sister.
Taunt: Aunt.
Voe: Nephew.

WHERE

Ah-co-tay: On the side of.
Ah-la-mair: At sea (shrimping).
Ah-lawn-vair: Inside out.
Ah-pray-pray: Almost; nearly.
Ah-tair: On shore.
Donh-nah-vonh: In front of.
Duh-boot: Standing up.
Duh-sue: On.
Ee-see: Here.
Ee-seed-donh: In here.
La: There.
La-bah: That thing over there.
Onh-bah: Down the bayou.
Onh-hoe: Up the bayou.
Onh-nod-yair: In back of.
Ont: In between.
Ont-day-yarr: Outside.
Ont-donh: Inside.
Ont-sue: Underneath.
Pod-duh-sue: On the bottom of.
Too-pot-too: All over; everywhere.

Slang and Silliness

A

Ack: The process of doing or performing something; act.

Acka-hall: Intoxicating liquor containing alcohol; alcohol.

Afta: Behind in place or order; after.

Ah-lure: The manner in which you comport yourself; an attitude.

Ah-vawn-say-ah-back: To go backward; (literally, to go forward in reverse).

Amma-nish-un: Things used in weapons; ammunition.

Anh: "No kidding!"

Anh: "What?" "How's that again?"

Ann-udder: An additional one; another.

At-leet: Someone who takes part in sports; athlete.

Aw-aw: Oh-oh; oops.

Awsh-turrs: Edible marine bivalve mollusks; oysters.

B

Babe-ull: Be able to.

Badeing: To wash in a tub; bathing.

Badeing-suit: What you wear to go swimming; bathing suit.

Bah-doom: An imitation of the sound that something big makes when it falls.

Bat: The act of washing; bath.

Bat-ray: A device that generates electrical current; battery.

Bat-tub: The place where you wash yourself; bath tub.

Behine: In back of; the rear; the behind; the buttocks.

Belly bus: A type of dive; a belly flop.

Bert: The beginning of existence; birth.

Bleeb: To accept as true or real; believe.

Bloon: An inflatable rubber bag; a balloon.

Boat or Bowf: The one and the other; both.

Booger-boo: A minor mistake; a small mess-up.

Bone-narrow: A bow and arrow, (this term usually refers only to the bow).

Boo-lye: A spotlight worn on the forehead, usually used for hunting at night.

Boom: One of the two outriggers extending outward from a shrimp boat which is used to pull or drag the trawls.

Boons: What the human skeletal frame is made up of; bones.

Boo-ree-flay: Flustered; angered; mad.

Breed: To inhale and exhale air; breathe.

Breen: What you think with (well, most of us anyway); brain.

Brett: The air inhaled and exhaled; breath.

Brodacious tah-tah's: A term referring to a well-developed area of a female's chest.

Brudder: A male having the same mother and father as another male; brother.

Brum: Something used to sweep with; broom.

C

Cang: A metal container; can.

Cat-lick: Of or pertaining to the Christen church; Catholic.

Caw: A form of transportation; a car.

Cheen: A series of metal links or rings connected together; chain.

Chimber pot: What they used when they didn't have indoor outhouses; chamber pot; pah-chawm.

Chimley: For smoke to escape through a furnace; chimney.

Chirren: Plural of child; children.

Choob: A hollow cylinder that conveys a fluid or gas and functions as a passage; tube.

Choo-choo: Disgusting to see, smell or touch; nasty.

Choon: A melody; tune.

Choony: What momma's got that daddy wants; vagina.

Choooooo: "Wow, ain't that something!"

Chooseday: The day following Monday; Tuesday.

Chu-chut: A term used when you can't think of the name of something that you're referring to.

Claught: A fabric or material; cloth.

Clime: To rise or move up; climb.

Clinker: The little brown spot in the bottom of your drawers.

Cong-oh: A water moccasin (snake). Also a term used to designate something that is extraordinarily big.

Cool-yoe-beans: "Wait a minute; be patient."

Coss: The price of something; cost.

Cuzz: Short for cousin or relative. Also, a shortened form of "because."

D

Dan: Apart from; except for; than.

Dane-druss: Able or apt to do harm; dangerous.

Dare: In that place; there.

Dat: Being the one singled out; that.

Day: The third person pronoun; they.

Day-gray: (You know that thing they give you when you finished school); degree.

De or Duh: The definite article; the.

Deeze: Plural of this; these.

Dem: The third person pronoun; them.

Den: At that time in the past; then.

Denniss: Someone who pulls your teeth; dentist.

Diss: The person or thing present; this.

Doe: Despite the fact that; though.

Doe-doe: To go to sleep.

Doo-fuss: An extremely dense, stupid person.

Doze: Plural of that; those.

Dreen: To cause liquid to go out from; drain.

Duma-flitch: That thing right there (this term is used when you can't think of the name of the thing that you're referring to).

E

Eader: The one or the other; either.

Empire: Someone who calls balls and strikes; an umpire.

Eye drop: A game in marbles where you take a marble, stand up and put the marble besides the eye and drop it into a cigar box with a hole in the top. The smaller the hole the bigger the payoff.

F

Fack: Something known with certainty; fact.

Fack-tray: A place where goods are manufactured; a factory.

Fass: Acting or moving quickly; fast. Also, to abstain from eating; fast.

Fedders: What covers birds and ducks; feathers.

Fie-yuh: To become ignited; fire.

Fine: To come upon by accident; find.

Fleem: A luminous mass of burning gas or vapor; flame.

Fline: Moving through the air as if with wings; flying.

Flow: The surface of a room where you stand on; floor.

Flungered: To screw up; fail (this term is formed by combining the two words "failed" and "blundered").

Fly-talk: A spray to kill mosquitoes, gnats and other insects; insecticide.

Fonky: Out of date; old fashioned.

Foress: A dense growth of trees; forest.

For-michael: A laminated plastic sheet; formica.

Fot: Expelled gas; fart.

Fraid: Filled with fear; afraid.

Fren: An associate or acquaintance; friend.

Frotch: An expression meaning "To hell with it!"

Frum: Beginning at a specific place or time; from.

Fudging: A term used in playing marbles meaning to cheat or go ahead of a designated line.

Fur-duh: More distant in time or degree; further.

Fwarr: Having loose bowels; diarrhea.

Fyock: A term used to mean "To hell with it."

G

Gaaaah: An exclamation used to designate something that is extraordinary; wow!

Geem: A way of amusing yourself; game.

Geem-warrens: The officials who enforce the wildlife and fisheries regulations; Game Wardens.

Glubb: A fitted covering for the hand; glove.

Goof-onh: A very awkward stupid person.

Gooooh: "Wow, ain't that something?"

Gratt: Scram; get out of here; scat.

Gree-gree: A Cajun hex or spell cast by someone, to wish another person bad luck.

Grinny: An older form of granny; grandmother.

Groat: An increase in number, form or value; growth.

Gunna': Will; going to; gonna.'

H

Hamma: A tool used to nail with; hammer.

Haw-lass: To beat a hasty retreat; to haul ass.

Helt: A state of well-being; health.

Hiss-tray: A narrative of events; history.

Hi-yuh: More loftier than; higher.

Hose pipe: A garden hose (with or without the nozzle).

Hue-Hippy-Long bridge: The Huey P. Long bridge crossing the Mississippi river in New Orleans.

Human-beans: Higher life forms; human beings.

Hurry-keen: A sever tropical storm; a hurricane.

I

Inna-choob: An inflatable tube inside some tires; inner tube.

It's not over until it's over. "Say-pah-fee-knee-avonk say fee-knee: It's not over until the fat lady has finished her song.

J

Juss: Exactly; precisely; just.

K

Kenna-garden: A class for children not yet old enough to enter the first grade; kindergarten.

Kep: The past tense of keep; kept.

Ket: A collection of money during church services.

Kine: A variety, sort or type; kind.

L

Lass: Being or coming after all others; last.

Leck-trissity: What comes from those wires on the telephone posts; electricity.

Ledder: A component of the alphabet; letter. Also something beginning with "Dear John."

Lick: An unusual or extraordinary event. Also, to commit a stupid act.

Lie-berry: A place where you check out books; library.

Lie-yuh: One who tells lies; liar.

Liff: To raise in condition, rank or esteem; lift.

Lil-bitty-bit: A very small amount.

Lon-motor: Something used to cut grass with; lawn mower.

Loose-bottles: Diarrhea; loose bowels.

Luh-monia: Chronic inflammation of the lungs; pneumonia.

M

Make some coins: To earn money.

Matt: The study of numbers; mathematics.

Maught: An insect similar to a butterfly; moth.

May: An exclamation of surprise meaning "What do you want me to do about it?"

May-nezz: A white dressing spread on sandwiches; mayonnaise.

May-nonh: "Of course not!" "No!"

May-yah: "Of course;" "Yes!"

Mee-noo: A domestic catcher of rats; cat.

Meer-uh: What you look into every morning while you brush your teeth and shave; mirror.

Mines: Belonging to me; mine.

Mine-nezz: Another way of pronouncing mayonnaise.

Moe-hobbit-talee: A great boxer; Muhammed Ali.

Moff or mout: The cavity that takes in food; mouth.

Mose: Greatest in number, or quantity; most.

Muh-mare: The ladies who are dad or mom's mother; grandmother.

Munt: One of the twelve divisions of a year; month.

Murtelize: To completely destroy; to kill beyond dead.

N

Neckid: Having no clothes on; naked.

Ness: Where a bird keeps its' eggs; nest.

Neutral: A rodent resembling a beaver; nutria.

Nick-nick: What momma and daddy do at night; intercourse.

Nooz-pape-uh: A daily or weekly publication containing news and other items; newspaper.

Nuttin': Not a thing; nothing.

O

On-uh-count-uh: A reason for; on account of.

Out-motor-boat: A boat with the motor mounted on the transom; an outboard.

P

Pa-chawm: A chamber pot; slop jar; chimber pot.

Pah-chow: The approximation of the sound that is made when someone or something dives into the water.

Pah-gocksh: The approximation of the sound that is made when someone or something is being hit.

Pan-tuh: A black leopard; panther.

Pat: A trail or track; path.

Pee-lay: To beat up real bad; to defeat in grand fashion.

Pee-nee-tawnce-yair: A prison; jail; penitentiary.

Pee-rogue: A Cajun canoe, (without the bow and stern sticking their noses in the air like a snob; pirogue.

Peesh-wet: A scrawny boy; similar to a pip-squeek; runt.

Pick-chuh: That thing of your driver's license that make you look like a criminal; picture.

Pie: An earlier form of godfather.

Pie-near: One who ventures into unknown territory; pioneer.

Pie-yow: An approximation of the sound a gun or rifle makes when it is fired.

Pinches: Those two things that crawfish and crabs bite with; claws; pincers.

Pip-squeek: A scrawny boy; similar to a peesh-wet.

Piss-oh-lee: A yellow flower that supposedly, if you touched them then you'd pee in the bed.

Plah-reen: A confection made with either almonds or pecans in a boiling sugar syrup until crisp; praline.

Pleen: Like a Boeing 747; airplane.

Plerry: The marsh land of South Louisiana (a term derived from the word "prairie").

Pluggin: An electrical outlet where you plug in your television or other electrical things; receptacle.

Pond-uh: A friend or buddy; partner.

Poon-tang: What momma and daddy do at night to make the bed shake so much (provided that they get the kids to sleep early enough); intercourse.

Poo-oo: Something smells bad.

Poot: Another way of saying "fot;" to fart.

Poo-wee: Something smells very, very bad.

Pow-duh: A white substance used as a cosmetic; what you sprinkle on a baby's behind when you change the diapers; powder.

Prazz: What you say when the pilot tells you that it's just a minor problem but to fasten your seat belts just in case; prayers.

Preece: A male member of the clergy, below a Bishop, but above a Deacon; Priest.

Pup-air: The men who are dad or mom's daddy; grandfather.

Q

Quaw-eed-uss: A powerful force (an oil field term).

Quawk-so-lay-yuh: A very stupid person who sits around passively and allows things to happen to him or her.

R

Reet: A ring or circle of flowers; wreath.

Rench: To wash lightly with water; rinse.

Ress: To take a break from doing something; rest.

Road-machine: A piece of equipment used to pave a new road or to repair an old one; a grader.

Roase: A chunk of meat that you put in the oven to cook; roast.

Rooned: To be totally destroyed; ruined.

Row-day: To go visiting (this term involves much more than just simply visiting), more like going around to a friend's house and visiting just for the sport of it or to gossip, rather than being at home tending to things that are necessary or more important.

Rubba-ban: An elastic, rubber loop; a rubber band.

Rum: An area separated by walls or partitions; a room.

Rye-cheer: In this spot; right here.

S

Sam-itch: Two or more slices of bread with meat, cheese or other things between them, with ketchup, mayonnaise, mustard or hot sauce added on; a sandwich.

Sanny Claws: The jolly fat man who brings you presents on Christmas Eve; Santa Clause.

Scad: Startled or frightened; scared.

Scootch: To move over; make room.

She: To make doo-doo.

Shee-wee: A firecracker that doesn't explode. Also, something that fizzles out.

Shevel: Something to dig with; shovel.

Shiffer-robe: A chest of drawers; chiffonier.

Shyea: Made doo-doo.

Simpany: A large orchestra designed for playing symphonic works; a symphony.

Slippsies: A term used in playing marbles, meaning "oops the marble slipped," which allows the person to take another shot.

Smay: A term used to mean getting rid of an unwanted pet, usually a cat or dog by bringing the pet for a ride and dropping it off in a strange neighborhood.

Smell pretty: A pleasing scent or aroma; perfume.

Smood: Having an even surface; smooth.

Sock-ah-pah-tot: A term referring to an overweight person (literally a sack of potatoes).

Sow-uh: Having a sharp, tart or tangy taste; sour.

Speeder-upper: A governor that increases or decreases the speed of a motor; throttle.

Splain: To define or make clear; explain.

Splosion: A sudden rapid, violent release of energy; explosion.

Stilson rench: A tool; a pipe wrench (sometimes referred to as a Monkey Wrench in the oilfield). A big, big stilson is often referred to as a "Blue MacGurder" because of its power.

Stinger-ree: A fish having a whip-like tail armed with a venomous spline; a sting ray.

Stoopid: Slow to understand; stupid.

Stow: A place where merchandise is offered for sale; store.

Stummick: Where all the food you eat goes to; stomach.

Sum-tin: An undetermined or unspecified thing; something.

T

Taut: Taught. Also, to have an idea or thought.

Tawk: To articulate in words; talk.

Taw-lett: How Cajuns pronounce "Commode."

Tay-tens: The human mammary glands; breasts.

Teary: A belief or principle guided by judgment; theory.

Tee: Little male (shortened from the original "pee-tee").

Teef: Someone who steals; thief.

Tee-neg: A term of affection meaning "dear little boy."

Teet: Little female; shortened from "pee-tit." Also, what you chew with; teeth.

Tella-foam: An instrument that you pick up and say "Hello, is that you?" Telephone.

Tenner-shoes: Tennis shoes.

Ter-lett: How half of the up-Nort people pronounce commode.

Terra-pay: To go in for counseling; therapy.

Terse: A sensation of dryness in the mouth related to a need or desire to drink; thirst.

The grapes of rats: A book called "The Grapes of Wrath."

Tick: The opposite of thin; thick.

Tie: The part of the leg between the hip and the knee; thigh.

Tink: To have an idea or thought; think.

Tink-yoe-self: To think yourself better than the other people who are around you; snob.

Toace: To heat and brown bread; toast.

Toll: The past tense of tell; told.

Tooner: A type of fish; tuna.

Toot: What you put under your pillow and hope that the tooth fairy is gonna' bring you a dollar; tooth.

Toot-ake: An aching pain on or in the tooth; toothache.

Toylett: How the rest of the up-Nort people say "commode."

Troat: Where the Adams Apple is located; throat.

Troot: Conforming to knowledge, fact or logic; truth.

Truss: To believe and have faith in someone; trust.

Tuh-mater: A red fruit; a tomato.

Tuh-pole-yun: A waterproof canvas used to cover and protect things from moisture; tarpaulin.

Tumble set: An acrobatic head-over-heels stunt; somersault.

Tun-duh: The sound you hear after the lightning flashes; thunder.

U

Udder: The remaining one of two or more; other.

Umpire State Billing: The Empire State Building.

Un-duh: In a lower position or place; under.

Un-duh-neat: In a place beneath or below; underneath.

W

Wace: To use thoughtlessly or carelessly; waste.

Wah-you-tottsy: An exclamation meaning "Wow-wee!"

Ware: At or in what place; where.

Wass: A flying insect that has a stinger on the business end; wasp.

Watch-uh-muh-call-it: That thing (another word used when you can't think of the name of the thing or person that you're referring to).

Waze or ways: A place where a boat is pulled up out of the water so that repairs or painting can be done; dry dock.

Wazz: A Cajun contraction; where is it?

Wedda: The state of the atmosphere at any given time or place; weather.

Wedda man: The guy or gal on TV who say there's going to be sunshine, then you better bring your umbrella 'cause it's probably gonna' rain; weather man; meteorologist.

Weel-barrel: A one or two wheeled vehicle with handles used to carry small, heavy loads; wheelbarrow.

Weeny: A smoked sausage made of pork or beef formed into long, reddish links; hot dog. Also, a term used to designate a wimp.

"When you feel froggy, leap:" "When you feel that you can take me on; when you feel that you can beat me, then go ahead and try." Sometimes used as a bluff.

Wile: A period of time; while.

Witt: As a comparison; with.

Wooz-ought or Woo-zawt: An alternative for "You all."

Wurt: The quality of something that makes it useful; worth.

Y

Yah: An affirmative reply; yes!

Yall: Not just you but the others with you; you all.

Yang-yang: The thing that hangs between a man's legs; penis.

Yoe: The possessive form of the pronoun "You;" your.

Yoot: The condition or quality of being young; youth.

Z

Zink: A water basin used to wash dishes in; sink.

Cajun Vocabulary Redux

Ah: As in bother, mop or yacht.
Ahl: As in Polly, collie or dolly.
Anh: As in ran land or tan.
Arr: As in car, par or mar.
Aud: As in laud, bawdy or pawed.
Aw: As in saw, gnaw or father.
Awl: As in crawl, doll or ball.
Awm: Ah in ohm, home or roam.
Awnt or Ront: As in daunt, gaunt or taunt.
Awsh: As in caution, awash or squash.
Awz: As in clause, pause or cause.
Bah: As in bayou, bottle or bother.
Bawn: As in brawn, lawn or dawn.
Buh: As in butter, butt or barrage.
Cah or Kah: As in cog, college or collar.
Caw: As in paw, awe or saw.
Cawm: As in pome, roam or loam.
Cawt: As in ought, caught or thought.
Craw: As in paw, crawfish or law.
Deux: As in heard, purple or pas de deux.
Dieu: As in girl, hurl, or pearl.
Du: As in do, who or coo.
Duh: As in veranda, rough or dud.
Eau or Eaux: As in Bureau, oh or know.

Ee: As in see, bee or three.
Eii: As in dill, figure or pill.
Ess: As in best, rest or mess.
Euh: As in but, burly or curly.
Eum: As in gum, sum or thumb.
Ev: As in heavy, levee or heaven.
Feuh: As in earth, early or surly.
Gah: As in God, mod or nod.
Guh: As in cut, but or pop.
Igg: As in big, fig or rig.
Jay: As in day, way or hay.
Kah: As in cop, comic or dodge.
Kai: As in lye, eye or pie.
Kawt: As in bought, sought or ought.
Kuhl: As in bull, wool or pull.
La: As in rah, ha or lob.
Mott: As in cot, sot or what.
Muh: As in justice, just or must.
Nu: As in nuclear, noose, or nude.
Nuh: As in but, cut or dud.
Ohm: As in comb, home or dome.
Oii: As in doing, booing or cooing.
Oin: As in coin, loin or join.
Onh: As in bone, gone or lone.
Ont or Awnt: As in want, haunt or taunt.
Oo: As in boot, toot or root.
Ought: As in caught, fought or moth.
Pah: As in pop, pocket or faux pas.
Poos: As in noose, moose or loose.
Rahl: As in collar, dollar or holler.
Roo: As in too, moo or coo.
Sah: As in cot, pah or hot.
Tood: As in you'd, rude or sued.
Uh: As in but, cut or hut.
Urr: As in purr, sir or cur.
Uzz: In does, buzz or fuzz.
Vii: As in vie, pie or tie.
Waw: As in patois, wasp or squaw.
Yea: As in pay, way or say.
Yuh: As in hut, but or cut.

FRENCH TO ENGLISH

A

A-banh: Well then; so.

Abb-ah-la-puss: Poison ivy.

A-care: A square (a carpenter's tool).

A-call: School.

A-clair: The flash before the thunder; lightning.

A-clair-see: Cleared up; lightened up.

A-coot: To give heed to; to listen to.

A-coo-tay: Gave heed to; listened to.

A-core-shay: To skin; scrape.

A-cray-viss: A crawfish.

A-cree: Wrote.

A-cree-blay: To beat up. Also, to destroy.

A-crozz: To smash.

A-crozz-zay: Smashed.

A-day: Helped; helping.

A-fyall: To squash.

A-fyall-lay: Squashed.

A-glizz: A church.

A-goll: Equal; even; level.

Ah: Has.

Ah-barr: On board; aboard.

Ah-bee-tood: A habit. Also an attitude.

Ah-bee-yea: To dress up; put on clothes.

Ah-bott: To take down; dismantle.
Ah-bue-tway: Get used to; become accustomed to.
Ah-sid: Acid.
Ah-co-tay: On the side.
Ah-crow-shay: Hooked.
Ah-fair: An affair. Also, a thing.
Ah-gray-yobb: Agreeable; easy going.
Ah-jourd-dwee: Today; this day.
Ah-la-mair: At sea.
Ah-lawn-vair: Inside out.
Ah-lay: Will go.
Ah-leem-met: An item used to start a fire; a match.
Ah-loss: In other words.
Ah-lume: To light.
Ah-lume-may: Lit.
Ahl-wet: Tonsils.
Ah-mee: Friend; companion.
Ah-more: Love.
Ah-pah: Bait; lure (fishing term).
Ah-pah-rawnce: Appearance.
Ah-pair-sue: To realize; to become aware of.
Ah-pause: To oppose; to go against.Ah-pell: To call.
Ah-play: Called.
Ah-poe-zay: Opposite; across from.
Ah-prawn-tee: An apprentice; beginner; novice.
Ah-prawsh: To approach.
Ah-pray: After.
Ah-prayed-manh: The day after tomorrow.
Ah-pray-mee-dee: The afternoon; after 12 noon.
Ah-pray-pray: Almost; nearly; just about.
Ah-pro-shay: Approached; came near.
Ah-roam-nay: Will return or bring something back.
Ah-rawnge: To arrange.
Ah-ray-tay: Stopped.
Ah-ree-vay: Arrived. Also, happened.
Ah-rett: To stop.
Ah-riv: To arrive. Also, to happen.

Ah-say: Enough.

Ah-say-yuh: To try; attempt.

Ah-say-yea: Tried; attempted.

Ah-stir: Now.

Ah-swarr: Tonight.

Ah-syett: A plate (to eat out of).

Ah-tair: On shore; ashore.

Ah tawn: To hear.

Ah-tawn-du: Heard.

Ah-tay: Went.

Ah-throp: To catch.

Ah-throp-pay: Caught.

Ah-tosh: To attach.

Ah-vawn: Before; in front of.

Ah-vawn-mee-dee: The morning; after midnight.

Ah-vawn-say: Advanced; went ahead; went forward.

Ah-vawnse: To advance; to go ahead; to go forward.

Ah-vay: Had.

Ah-veck: With.

Ah-viss: A screw.

Ah-voe-kah: A lawyer.

Ah-vreel: April.

Ah-war: To have.

Ah-woo: August.

A-glizz: A church.

A-kahl: Shells (usually of crab, shrimp, or crawfish).

A-kell: Which?

Am: To like.

Am-bay-sill: An imbecile; a stupid person.

A-modge-in: Imagine.

A-modge-ee-nay: Imagining.

A-more-witt: Hemorrhoids.

Am-poe-sib: Impossible.

Am-poor-taunt: Important.

An: The number, "one." Also, "A."

A-nay: Born; birth.

Anh: "You don't say!"

Anh: "What's that you say?"

Anh-dee-mee-urr: A half an hour.

Anh-duze-yam: A second.

Anh-fwaw: One time; once.

An-mee-nuht: A minute.

Annie-moe: An animal. Also, cattle.

An-ought: Another.

An-ought-fwaw: Another time.

An-ought-shawz: Another thing; something else.

An-soolt: To insult.

An-sool-tay: Insulted.

An-sue-rawnce: Insurance.

An-three: A messy female.

A-pang: A pin.

A-paul: A shoulder.

A-pay: Thick.

A-pie-yea: To scatter; spread about.

A-preeve-yea: A castnet.

Arr-jonh: Money.

Arr-poe-zay: To rest; to take a break.

A-schway (a nautical term): Stuck; aground.

A-shawnge: Coins.

A-shawn-juh: Changed.

A-sheen-nay: Tired; worn out.

A-shell: A ladder.

A-shop: To get loose; to escape. Also, to drop.

A-shop-pay: Got loose; got away; escaped. Also, dropped.

A-show-day: To scald.

A-show-fay: Chafed.

A-show-kay: To make angry; made angry.

A-tah: A state.

A-tair-nay: To sneeze; sneezed.

A-tan: Unlit.

A-tanh: To unlight; to put out; extinguish.

A-tay: The summer.

A-three-pay: Gutted.

A-toff: Material; cloth; fabric.

A-tood-yea: To study.

A-toof: To smother; asphyxiate; suffocate.

A-toof-fay: Smothered; asphyxiated; suffocated.

A-traught: Narrow.

A-trawn-jay: A stranger.

A-throng-glay: To choke; choking. Also, to strangle.

A-twall: A star.

A-vawn-tie: A fan (to cool things off).

Avon-wee: Fainted; passed out.

Avon-weer: Faint; pass out.

Awn-ghee: An eel.

Awn-glay: English.

Awn-nay: A year.

Awn-nay-pah-say: The last year.

Awn-nay-pro-shan: Next year.

Awn-net: Honest; truthful.

Awn-too-rodge: A wall.

Awss: Bones.

Aye-ya-yie: What you yell for a major hurt.

Aye-yie: What you yell for a minor hurt.

A-you: Where; in what place?

A-zay: Easy; simple.

B

Bah: Low.

Bahl: A dance.

Bahl-yea: A broom; sweeping.

Bah-nawn: A banana.

Bahr-yair: A fence.

Bah-sin: An oven.

Bah-tard: A bastard; an illegitimate son.

Bah-tear: Building; will build.

Bah-tee: Built. Also, fought.

Bah-three: A battery.

Bah-tie: A fight or battle. Also, a Cajun card game.

Bah-toe: A boat.

Bah-tonh: A stick.

Bah-vay: To drool.

Bah-zawn-nay: Freckled.

Ball: A bowl.

Ban-yea: Took a bath. Also, a beignet.

Barb-bue: A catfish.

Bare-suzz: A rocker.

Bare-wet: A wheelbarrow.

Bar: The side.

Bar-ah-draught: The right side.

Bar-ah-gawsh: The left side.

Baum: A pot to cook in.

Bawn: A tire. Also, good. Also, was better.

Bawn-dieu: The good Lord; God.

Bawn-ess-pree: Good sense; sane.

Bawn-kett: A sidewalk.

Bawn-mod-shay: Cheap; low priced.

Bawn-urr: Early.

Bay-bay: An infant; baby.

Bay-bell: A toy.

Bay-bet: An insect.

Bay-say: Lowered.

Bay-thrauv: Beets.

Bay-tie: A beast; (sometimes refers to cattle).

Bay-tizz: Foolishness.

Bee-god-noo: A sea snail.

Bee-yea: A bill; paper money.

Be-knee: Blessed; holy; sacred.

Bell-surr: Sister-in-law.

Ben: Beans.

Bess: Lower.

Bet-rouge: Red bug.

Bet: Silly; foolish.

Biss-quee: A biscuit.

Blauk: A block. Also, to block.

Blawn: A blond.

Blawn-kett: A blanket.

Blay-say: To bless. Also, to wound.

Blett: A mink.

Blogg: A type of jellyfish.

Blow-kay: Blocked; got in the way of.

Bob: A beard.

Bode-durr: Border; edge.

Bog: A ring (for the finger).

Bonh-kett: A sidewalk.

Bonk: A bank.

Boo: Mud.

Boo-cawn: Smoke.

Boo-cawn-nay: Smoked; smoking.

Boo-coo: Plenty; a whole lot of.

Bood-anh: A kind of Cajun sausage made of pork, rice and other ingredients.

Boo-day: To pout.

Boo-duzz: One who pouts; pouter.

Boog: A boy.

Boo-klett: Curls (in the hair).

Boo-lonh: A bolt.

Boo-ray: A Cajun card game; (bourre').

Boosh: The mouth. Also, to stop up; plug up.

Boo-shay: Stopped up; plugged up.

Boosh-onh: A stopper; a fishing cork.

Boot: The end.

Boot-onh: A button; to button.

Boo-yea: Boiled.

Boo-yee: Flour, milk and egg pudding; pap.

Bosk-you-luzz: Boisterous.

Bought: Boots.

Bow: Good looking; pretty; beautiful.

Bow-bow: A sore; a wound.

Bow-frair: Brother-in-law.

Bow-gay: A buggy.

Bra: The arm; arms.

Bra-get: A zipper on a trouser.

Bra-vuh: Brave.

Brawsh: A brush.

Bree-yont: Brilliant. Also, shiny. Also, bright.

Bree-yea: Shined; shone.

Brew-low: Gnats.

Brew-lure: A burn.

Brew-yodd: Fog.

Brizz: A breeze.

Bross: To kiss. Also, to stir.

Bross-say: Kissed. Also, stirred.

Bruel: To burn.

Brew-lay: Burned; burnt; burning.

Bue: Drank.

Buff: A bull.

Burr: Butter.

Buzz-wanh: To need.

Bwarr: Drinking fluids.

Bwaw: To drink. Also, wood. Also, a tree.

Bwaw-sonh: Liquor; an alcoholic drink.

Bway: A buoy.

Bwett: A box.

Bye: A tub.

Bye-ah-la-vay: A wash tub (used before indoor plumbing).

Bye-yea: Yawned.

C

Cah-goo: Feeling faint and weak.

Call: To stick to; adhere.

Caud: A rope.

Caught: The ribs. Also, the neighborhood.

Cawm: Like; as; seemingly.

Cawm-awnce: To begin; start.

Cawm-awn-say: Began; started.

Cawm-mee-yonh: Communion.

Cawm-onh: How?

Cawm-pah: A compass.

Cawm-pawn-yee: A company. Also, to have visitors.

Cawm-prawn: To understand.

Cawm-pree: Understood.

Cawm-unh: Common; plain; ordinary.

Cawn: A cane.

Cawn-dee: Candy.

Cawn-nay: To know.

Cawn-net: Will know.

Cawn-nu: Knew.

Cawn-sair: Cancer.

Cawn-sonh: Drawers; underwear.

Cawn-stee-pay: Constipated.

Cawnt: To count. Also, against.

Cawn-taunt: Glad; happy.

Cawn-tay: Counted.

Cawn-tee-noo: To continue.

Cawn-tee-tay: Quite a few; many.

Cawnt-war: A counter (as in a kitchen or restaurant).

Cease: The number six.

Cease-tawm: A system.

Cell-a-bray: To celebrate; celebrated.

Chan: Held; holding.

Chanh: To hold.

Chross: Dirt; filth.

Chrutt: A crust. Also, having a thick coating of dirt or filth.

Chu: The behind; derriere.

Chu-rouge: Angry or irritated (literally the red ass).

Clair: Clear.

Clawsh: A bell.

Clay: A key.

Clue: A nail. Also, a boil.

Cob: Cable (a nautical term).

Cob-awn: A shack. Also, a playhouse.

Cob-oh-say: Battered; used; worn out.

Cob-ree: A goat.

Co-cawm: A cucumber.

Coco-dree: A crocodile.

Cod-a: A square. Also to be square.

Cod-lay: A dip net.

Cod-nah: A padlock.

Co-fair: Why?

Coin yea: To knock.

Coke-eii: Oyster shells.

Coke-leush: The croup.

Co-lair: Anger; temper.

Co-lay: To lean against. Also, stuck to; adhered. Also, to hit someone or something really hard.

Co-leck-syonh: A collection in church.

Co-ledge: College.

Cole-yea: A necklace.

Coll: To sink. Also, the compartment where shrimp are iced on a shrimp boat.

Coll-ah-mah: A squid.

Coll-lay: Sank.

Coll-lee-tay: A kind; sort; type.

Coll-mee: Calmed down.

Coll-meer: Calming down.

Co-loy: An alcoholic drink.

Con-ahl: A canal.

Cong-oh (a snake): A water moccasin.

Conh-yea: Knocked.

Coo: The neck. Also, some big event or happening.

Coo-bee-yonh: A sauce piquant with less spice and beginning with a roo.

Cood: To sew.

Cood-nor: A norther (literally, a lick from the north).

Cood-pyea: A kick (literally, a lick from the foot).

Cood-top: A slap.

Cool: To leak.

Coo-lay: Leaked.

Coo-lurr: Color.

Cool-war: A colander.

Coor: To run. Also, a yard or lawn.

Coo-ree: Ran.

Coo-rear: Running.

Coo-rodge: Courage.

Coor-say: Chased; chasing.

Coort: Short.

Coose: On the run; the chase.

Coosh: A diaper. Also, to lie down to sleep.

Coo-shay: To go to bed.

Coo-tow: A knife.

Coo-vair: A cover.

Coo-vair-tour: A covering.

Coo-yawn: A silly female.

Coo-yonh: A silly male.

Coo-yonh-nay: Tricked.

Coo-yonh-nod: Foolishnes.

Cop-ee-tahl: Capitol.

Cop-ee-tan: A captain.

Cop-oh: A coat.

Cop-oh-see-day: A raincoat.

Cop-oh-tay: To turn over; to capsize.

Co-reck: Correct; right.

Corn: Horn.

Cot: The number four. Also, a card.

Cot-awz: The number fourteen.

Co-tay: The side.

Cot-oh-lick: A catholic.

Cot-ruh-vanh: The number eighty (literally, four twenties).

Cot-ruh-vanh-diss: The number ninety.

Cot-toosh: Shells; ammunition; cartridges.

Coup: A cut; to cut. Also, narrow space for a boat to pass in.

Cram: Cream. Also, ice cream.

Craw: To think. Also, a snob. Also, a cross.

Crawsh: Crooked or bent; not straight.

Cray-dee: Credit.

Cray-vay: Died.

Cray-yonh: A pencil.

Cree: To write. Also, a cry or yell.

Cree-mee-nahl: A criminal.

Crease-muss: Christmas.

Cree-yea: Shouted out; cried out; yelled.

Crev: To die.

Crew-tay: Encrusted.

Crizz: A craze or fad. Also, to throw a fit or temper tantrum.

Crobb: A crab. Also, a slow poke.

Crobb-mall: A soft shelled crab.
Crock: A crack; to crack.
Crock-ben: Fully crazy.
Cromp: A-"U"-shaped nail.
Croot: Filth.
Croo-tay: Filthy.
Crop-oh: A frog.
Crow-she: Bent; hooked; dented.
Cur: The heart.

D

Dah-barr: Providing; contingent upon.
Dahl: A gutter.
Dah-la: Someone who is silly; foolish.
Dan-yair: The last one.
Dan-yea: Final.
Dare-yair: The behind; posterior.
Darr: Asleep; to sleep.
Dawm: A queen.
Dawm-ett: Flannel material.
Dawm-odge: Damage.
Dawn: To give.
Dawn-ah-vonh: In front of.
Dawn-an-alonh: In a while; after while.
Dawnce: To dance; a dance.
Dawn-jay: Danger.
Dawn-nay: Gave.
Dawn-tiss: A dentist.
Dawss: A dose.
Day: Some.
Day-bawsh: To knock off from work.
Day-bow-shay: Knocked off from work.
Day-brang-gay: Dismantled; broken up.
Day-coo-rah-jay: Discouraged.
Day-crawsh: Unhook.
Day-crow-shay: Unhooked.
Day-fair: Undoing. Also, to be rid of.
Day-fawm: Females; women.

Day-fawn: To defend.

Day-fawn-say: Busted. Also, used to designate someone with an extraordinary capacity for food; glutton.

Day-fawnse: Defense.

Day-fay: To undo; undid.

Day-fay-sill: Picky; choosy.

Day-fwaw: Sometimes.

Day-gull-lay: To vomit; to throw up.

Day-jah: Already.

Day-jan-nay: Breakfast.

Day-leave-ray: Delivered.

Day-lee-cot: Delicate.

Day-liv: To deliver.

Day-low-jay: To move; to change residence.

Day-mawnge: To itch; itching.

Day-mawn-jay: Itched.

Day-mawn-jay-zawn: Itchiness.

Day-pawn: To depend on.

Day-pawnse: To spend; an expenditure.

Day-pawn-say: Spent.

Day-pay-shay: Hurry.

Day-pue: Since.

Day-sawm: December.

Day-sawn: To descend; to come down.

Day-see-day: Decided.

Day-shar-jay: Discharged.

Day-shear: To tear; to rip.

Day-she-ray: Tore; ripped.

Day-vee-say: Unscrewed.

Day-viss: To unscrew.

Day-voe-ray: Devoured (usually refers to someone who is famished and is devouring his food).

Day-zear: To desire.

Day-zee-ray: Desired.

Daze-onh-urr: A disgrace; dishonor.

Dee: To tell; to say; said. Also, the number ten.

Deece: Ten.

Deece-tawnce: Distance.

Dee-mawnsh: Sunday.

Dee-nay: Dinner; to have dinner.

Dee-pyoss: Ten dollars.

Deer: Will tell.

Dee-shwaw: Some fun; some excitement.

Dee-soo: Ten cents.

Dee-too: At all (usually preceded by "not" or "nothing").

Dee-varce: Divorce.

Deex-yawn-air: A dictionary.

Deez-nuff: The number nineteen.

Deez-set: The number seventeen.

Deez-wit: The number eighteen.

Deuce-monh: Slow.

Deuh: The number two.

Deuh-manh: Tomorrow; the next day.

Deuh-manh-oh-swarr: Tomorrow night.

Diss: The number ten.

Diss-put: To fuss. Also, a dispute; a fight; to argue.

Diss-pue-tay: Fussed.

Do: Sweet.

Doak-turr: A doctor; physician.

Dodge-noo: On your knees; kneeling.

Doe: The back.

Doob: Double.

Dooce: Is sweet.

Door-mere: Sleeping.

Doot: To doubt.

Doo-tay: Doubted.

Dooze: The number twelve.

Doo-zan: A dozen.

Drah: A sheet (linen).

Draught: Straight.

Draught-la: Right there; in that place.

Drawl: Strange.

Dree-guy: Trash.

Dud-throw: Too much.

Due-ray: Lasted.

Duh-boot: Standing on your feet.

Duh-qwaw: Something.

Duh-sue: On.

Durr: Hard.

Dwaw: Finger.

Dyob: The devil. Also, A fish similar to a sting ray.

E

Ed: To help.

Ee: He; him.

Ee-boo: An owl.

Ee-day: The mind. Also, an idea; a thought.

Ee-let: A small island.

Ee-nonh-mooi: Plentiful (raining the item being referred to).

Ee-see: Here; right in this place.

Ee-seed-donh: In here; inside.

Ee-vair: The winter.

Ee-voe: A level (carpenter's tool).

Eleck-three-see-tay: Electricity.

Ell: Her; she.

Ell-mam: Herself.

Ell-vay: Raised; reared.

Ess: The East.

Ess-cawn-dahl: A scandal.

Ess-coll-yea: Steps; stairs.

Ess-pair: To wait.

Ess-pay-ray: Waited.

Ess-peon-nay: To stick your nose in someone else's business. Also to instigate.

Ess-peon-urr: A person who sticks his nose in somebody else's business; a busybody.

Ess-pray: Especially. Also, on purpose.

Ess-pree: Sense. Also, a spirit.

Ess-pwarr: Ambition; aspiration.

Ess-tawm-ah: The stomach.

Ess-throw-pyea: Deformed; disabled or injured to the point of being handicapped.

Ess-tow-rah: A restaurant.
Ett: Will be.
Ex-cuzz: An excuse.
Ex-kwee-zay: Exquisite; very good.
Ex-plea-kay: Explained.
Ex-plick: Explain.
Ex-ploze-zay: Exploded.
Ex-q-zay: To excuse.
Ex-see-tah-syonh: Excitement.
Ex-see-tay: Excited.
Ex-trah: Extra.
Ex-zaum-men: To examine.
Ex-zaum-mee-nay: Examined.
Ex-zock-tee-monh: Exactly.
Ezz: Ease.

F

Fah-rin: Flour.Fah-shay: Angry; mad.
Fah-tee-cawnt: Tiresome.
Fah-tee-kay: Fatigued; tired.
Fah-tick: To tire; fatigue.
Fair: Will do. Also, iron; steel.
Fall: A crazy female.
Far: A force; to force.
Fawm: A woman; lady.
Fawn: To melt.
Fawn-du: Melted.
Fay: To do; did. Also, the top.
Fay-ah-crawr: To make believe; pretend.
Fay-dee-moll: To hurt; to be hurt.
Fay-purr: To scare.
Fay-ross: Ferocious.
Fay-zurr: A doer; one who does.
Fay-zurr-duh-mawn-three. A liar; someone who tells lies.
Fee-foe-lay: A spirit; marsh gas.
Fee-gurr: A face.
Fee-lay: To separate the meat of a fish from the bones; fillet. Also, finely ground sassafras leaves to make gumbo.

Fee-near: Finishing.

Fee-nee: To finish; finished.

Fee-sell: String.

Fess: The buttocks.

Fet: A holiday. Also, your birthday.

Feum: To smoke (cigars, or cigarette).

Fev: Peas.

Fev-plot: Butterbeans.

Fev-ree-yea: February.

Few-zee: A rifle or shotgun.

Fie: To feel dizzy or faint.

Fill: String. Also, often used to designate trawl webbing.

Filled-nan-yea: A spider web; cobwebs.

Finish: Fee-knee.

Fin-near: Will finish.

Flah-tooze: Flatter.

Flaught: To float.

Flawm: Flame.

Flee-jay: Crippled; lame.

Flot-ooze: Flattering.

Flow-tay: Floated.

Flurr: A flower.

Fly-yea: To strike or hit someone or something.

Fly-yea-anh-cood top: To slap.

Fock-three: A factory.

Foe-fee-lay: To make a temporary patch in a trawl.

Foe-rah: Could; must.

Foe-ray: The forest.

Fonh: The butt. Also, the bottom of something.

Fonh-chock: Cocky; smart; arrogant.

Foo: A crazy male.

Foo-net: Completely crazy.

Foo-guy-urr: A digger; a forager.

Foo-guy-yea: To dig; to forage.

Foo-tu: Finished; beaten; to have lost.

Foo-yea: Digging; dug.

Foo-yurr: One who digs.

Fought: Fault.

Four-shett: A fork.

Foy-yea: A fireplace.

Frah-geel: Fragile.

Frair: Brother.

Fram: To close.

Fram-may: Closed.

Fraud: Was cold.

Fraught: To rub; to lean against.

Frawm-mee: Ants.

Frawm-modge: Cheese.

Fray: Cool; chilly. Also, fresh.

Fray-cawnt: Frequent; often.

Freak-ah-say: A stew.

Free: Fried.

Free-moose: A frown; making faces.

Free sonh: Trembling; goose bumps; the chills.

Free-zett: Short, curly hair.

Froat-war: A wash board (used before washing machines).

Fronh-say: French.

Froo: Fruit.

Froo-froo: A careless, awkward person.

Frop-dah-barr: A sand fly.

Fro-tay: Rubbed.

Fwaw: A time. Also, the liver.

G

Gah-lair: A plainer (a carpenter's tool).

Gah-lawn-say: Swinging.

Gah-lett: A small, one layer cake.

Gah-lawnse: A swing.

Gah-rawn-tee: To guarantee.

Gah-rawsh: To throw.

Gah-row-shay: Threw; throwing.

Gah-tay: Spoiled. Also, rotten.

Gah-zett: A newspaper.

Gair: A war.

Gamm: To gamble.

Gamm-blay: Gambled.

Gamm-blurr: A gambler.

Gar-mawn-jay: A safe (a place where dishes and other eating utensils are kept). (Literally, "look food."). Known to non-Cajuns as a sideboard or hutch.

Gar-sonh: A boy. Also, a son.

Gaudge: The throat.

Gawsh: Awkward. Also, the left.

Gay-rear: To heal; cure.

Gay-ree: Healed; cured.

Gay-tay: Watched; will watch.

Geez-yea: The gizzard.

Gep: A wasp.

Get: To watch.

Ghom-bow: A gumbo. Also, okra.

Gimm: A game.

Glaub: A light bulb. Also, a globe.

Glee-sawnt: Slippery.

Glee-say: Slipped.

Gliss: To slip; to slide.

Gloss: Ice.

Gloss-say: Icy.

Gloss-yair: An ice box; refrigerator.

Go-blay: A goblet.

Gob-moosh: A flycatcher.

God: To keep. Also, to look at.

God-day: Kept. Also, looked at or looked for.

God-lee: A porch.

God-nod: Maypops.

God-noo-shett: Athlete's foot.

Goin: Win.

Goin-yea: Won.

Goll: The mange.

Goll-fay-tay: To caulk a boat to keep it from leaking.

Goll-fett: Caulked a boat.

Gonff: Bloated; full.

Gon-flay: To swell up; bloat; to puff up.

Gonh: A glove.

Goof-onh: An extremely stupid person.

Goor-monh: A greedy person.

Goor-mawn-dizz: Greediness.

Goot: A small taste.

Goo-tay: Tasted.

Goo-vair-nuh-monh: The government.

Goo-vair-nurr: A governor (mechanical and political).

Goo-vair-nye: To steer.

Goss-pee-yea: To waste; wasted.

Got-tow: Cake.

Gozz: Gas; gasoline.

Grah: Fat; plump.

Grah-fee-yea: Scratched.

Grah-nod: Another way of saying maypop.

Grah-vwaw: Gravel; shells.

Gramp: To climb; to ascend.

Gramp-pay: Climbed; ascended.

Granh: A squall.

Granh-noss-say: Drizzled; drizzling.

Gransh: To pout.

Gran-shay: Pouted.

Gran-shurr: Pouter; one who pouts.

Gran-yea: An attic.

Gray-say: Greased.

Gree-gree: A Cajun hex.

Gree-yea: To burn food.

Gree-yoe: A crumb; a small speck.

Greg-ah-cah-fay: A coffee pot.

Gress: Grease; to grease.

Grew-yea: Moved.

Groan: A big male.

Groan-mare: Grandmother.

Groan-pair: Grandfather.

Grodd-you-way: Graduate.

Grooi: To move.

Grop-anh: Grapnel.

Gross: A fat, plump female.

Gross-ree: Groceries.

Grott: To scratch. Also, the burnt part from the bottom of a pot or pan.

Grott-tay: Scratched.

Grow: A fat, plump male.

Grown: A big female.

Gwaw-lett: A schooner (a large shrimp boat).

Gwaw-lonh: A seagull.

H

Hah-lay: Pulled.

Hah-yee-sob: To be mischievous.

Haunt: To embarrass; to be embarrassed.

Hawnsh: The hip.

Hawsh: A hatchet.

Hawt: Was high.

Hees-twarr: History.

Heg: Sour; spoiled.

Heg-ree: Soured.

Hoe: Is high.

Holl: To pull.

I

Ill: An island.

Ill-me: An enemy.

J

Jah-loo: A jealous male.

Jah-looz: A jealous female.

Jan: To bother. Also, young.

Jan-nay: Bothered.

Jaub: A job.

Jew: Play.

Jhawn: Yellow.

Jhett: To buy. Also, to throw.

Jhnoo: The knee; knees.

Jhom: The leg; legs.

Jhom-bah-lye-ya: Jambalaya.

Jhom-bonh: A ham.

Jhom-may: Never.

Jhon-siv: The gums.

Jhue-day: Cursed.

Jhuh-dee: Thursday.

Jhuss: Just; exact. Also; fair.

Jhway: Played; playing.

Jod-danh: A garden.

Joe-lee: Pretty.

Jong: To think.

Jong-lay: Thought; thinking.

Jonh-vee-yea: January.

Jop: To bark.

Jop-pay: Barked; barking.

Jour: The daytime.

Jull: The mouth. Also, to cry.

Jull-lay: Cried; crying.

June-nay: A day.

Jurr: To curse.

Jwanh: June.

Jweel-yea: July.

K

Kah-goo: Pale; looking faint.

Kah-lawt: A slap.

Kah-low-tay: Slapped; slapping.

Kah-nahl: A canal. Also, a ditch.

Kah-narr: A duck.

Kah-narr-fronh-say: A French duck; mallard.

Kah-nick: A marble.

Kah-nush: A cane reed.

Kah-nye: Smart; slick; tricky.

Kah-pop: Capable; able.

Kah-priss: Caprice; malice.

Kah-ram: The Lenten season.

Kah-rawnt: The number forty.

Kah-say: Broke; broken.

Kah-shay: To hide; hidden.

Kah-shett: In hiding. Also, on the sly; behind the back.

Kah-tay-shiss: Catechism.

Kah-wan: A sea turtle.

Kah-zock: Crazy; someone wild and overly foolish.

Kai-monh: An alligator.

Kai-you: A small rock; pebble.

Kay-can: Someone.

Kay-can-dawt: Someone else.

Keel-yair: A spoon.

Kess: A case.

Ket: A collection taken up in church.

Key: What? or What!

Key-tay: Left behind.

Key-ya: "What's wrong?" "What's the matter?"

Kick-shawz: Something.

Kick-shawz-dawt: Something else.

Kit: To leave. Also, to let; allow.

Knee: Neither.

Ko-maud: A toilet.

Ko-shawn: A female pig.

Ko-shonh: A male pig.

Koss: A cap. Also, to break.

Koss-bore-go: A sheepshead (a fish).

Koss-tet: A hatchet.

Krah-vott: A necktie; a cravat.

Kree-kett: A cricket.

Krimm: A crime.

L

La: There. Also, "the" (singular).

La-bah: Over there.

La-Chrish-Ten: Santa Clause.

La-jaub: The mumps.

La-lawm: The waves.

La-luze-yan: Louisiana.

La-myan: Mine.

Lan-dee: Monday.

Lange: Clothes.

Lange-daunt-sue: Underwear.

La-pan: Sorrow; grief.
La-panh: A rabbit.
La-shay: To let go; set free.
La-stick: Elastic.
La-tyanh: Yours.
La-vay: To wash; washed; washing.
La-vett: A bath towel
Lawm: A blade (to cut with).
Lawn-fair: Hell; the opposite of heaven.
Lawn-manh: The day after tomorrow.
Lawn-say: Throbbed.
Lawn-tawn-pah-say: Long ago; in the distant past.
Lawt: The other one.
Lay: "The" (plural). Also, milk.
Lay-jay: Light; not heavy.
Lay-lamb: Tears; crying.
Lay-sawnce: Perfume.
Lay-tu: Lettuce.
Lay-zawt: The others; those.
Lee: A bed. Also, to read.
Lee-mitt: Limit.
Lee-monh: Lemon.
Leem-onh-nod: Lemonade.
Leem-yair: A light (such as a light bulb or flashlight).
Lee-net: Eyeglasses.
Lee-onh: A lion.
Leer: Reading.
Lee-shay: Licked.
Lees-odd: A lizard.
Lee-swance: A license.
Less: To let; to allow.
Let: A letter (as in "Dear John"). Also, a letter of the alphabet.
Lev: The lips. Also, to raise.
Lev-nay: A snob.
Lim: A file.
Ling: A line. Also, a fishing rod or pole.
Lish: To lick.

Liv: A pound. Also, a book.

Lock: A lake.

Lodge: Wide.

Loll-waw: The law; the sheriff.

Lomp: A lamp.

Long: The tongue.

Lonh: Long.

Lonh-tonh-pah say: A long time ago.

Loomer-oh: A number.

L'orr: Gold.

Lot-donh: In there; inside.

Louce: Loose.

Lourd: Heavy.

Low-durr: An odor; an unpleasant smell; to stink.

Low-kay: The hiccups.

Luh-pranh-tonh: The spring.

Lune: The moon.

Lu-tay: To wrestle; wrestled.

Lwanh: Far.

Lwaw: The law; a law.

Lwee: He; him.

Lwee-mam: Himself.

Lye: Garlic.

M

Mag-nee-fick: Magnificent.

Mah: A mask. Also, a mast on a boat.

Mah-cock: A monkey.

Mah-dawm: Madam; Mrs.

Mah-gah-zin: Magazine.

Mah-la-dee: A sickness.

Mah-lan: A sneaky, tricky female.

Mah-lanh: A sneaky, tricky male.

Mah-lease-yeuh: Malicious.

Mah-lod: To be sick.

Mah-liss: Malice.

Mahr: A marshy inlet; a pond.

Mah-ran: Godmother; nanny.

Mah-rawn: Wild; not domesticated.

Mah-ray: The tide.

Mah-ree: A husband. Also. To marry.

Mahrse: March.

Mahr-yea: Married.

Mah-shin: A machine.

Mah-tanh: The morning.

Make-ruh-dee: Wednesday.

Mam: Alike.

Mam-shawz: The same thing.

Manh: The hand.

Man-wee: Midnight.

Manse: Thin; skinny.

Mare: Mother. Also, the womb. Also, the sea or body of water.

Mare-see: Thanks.

Mar-shay: Marched; walked.

Mawn: People.

Mawn-ee-fick: Terrific; magnificent; really good.

Mawnge: To eat.

Mawn-jay: Ate; eating. Also, food.

Mawn-kay: To miss; missed.

Mawnsh: A handle.

Mawn-sull: By myself; alone.

Mawnt: To show. Also, a watch. Also, to tell a lie.

Mawn-thray: Showed; shown.

Mawn-three: A lie.

Mawn-turr: A liar; one who lies.

Mawn-yair: A way.

May: To put. Also, the month of May.

May-die: A medal.

May-lay: Mixed; tangled.

May-lodge-monh: An entanglement.

May-nodge: Furniture.

May-pree-zay: To speak bad about someone.

May-ree-tay: Merited; earned.

May-thress: A teacher.

May-thress-day-call: A school teacher.

May-zone: A house; a home.

Mee: Did put.

Mee-dee: Twelve o'clock; noon.

Meel yawn: A million.

Meel-yeuh: The middle; center.

Mee-nurr: A minor; an under age person.

Meer-war: A mirror.

Meese-yeuh: Mister; Mr.

Meez-air: Trouble.

Mee-zee-rob: Miserable.

Meg: Skinny; to be lean.

Mel: To mix.

Me-rock: A miracle.

Mess: A church function; Mass.

Met: Will put.

Mill: A thousand. Also, a mile.

Mitt-sin: Medicine.

Mnu: Came.

Mock: A mark; to mark.

Mock-ah-cree: A mockery; monkeyshines.

Mock-ah-roan-nee: Macaroni; spaghetti.

Mock-crow: A gigolo.

Mod-ah-gwanh: A mosquito.

Mod-dee: Tuesday.

Mod-dee-grah (literally, fat Tuesday): Mardi Gras.

Mod-ree-yea: A creosote board.

Moe: A word.

Moe-chay: Half.

Moe-vay: Bad. Also, a mean male.

Moe-vay-ess-pree: A mean spirit.

Moe-vezz: A mean female.

Mogga-zanh: A store.

Moll: Did wrong. Also, bad. Also, a male. Also, the mail.

Moll-ah-dee: Malady; a sickness.

Moll-ah-deed-curr: Heart trouble.

Moll-ah-jawn-thray: Disheveled; sloppy.

Moll-cawm-pree: Misunderstood.

Moll-duh-mair: Seasickness.
Moll-duh-tet: A headache.
Moll-oh-curr: To be nauseous.
Moll-oh-donh: A toothache.
Moll-oh-vaunt: A stomach ache.
Monh: Me; myself; I.
Monh-tonh: The chin.
Monk: To miss.
Moo: Soft.
Moo-dee: Damned; cursed; no good; foul.
Moose: Moss.
Moose-tick: A mosquito.
Moose-tosh: A mustache.
Moosh: A fly.
Moosh-ah-myell: A honey bee.
Moosh-war: A handkerchief.
Moo-tard: Mustard.
Moo-tonh: A sheep.
Moo-yea: Raining; rained.
Mord: To bite; will bite.
More-so: A piece; a part.
Mort: Dead.
Mosque: A mask.
Mossock: Massacre; damage.
Mossock-cray: Massacred; damaged.
Mot-lah: A mattress.
Mot-low: A deckhand (usually on a shrimp boat).
Mott-toe: A hammer.
Muh-mair: Grandmother.
Muh-yurr: Better.
Mu-lay: A mule.
Murr: A blackberry.
Muy-nwarr: A black mullet (a fish).
Mu-zick: Music.
Mwanh: Minus.
Mwanse: Less.
Mwaw: A month.

Mwaw-pass-say: Last month.

Mwaw-pro-shan: Next month.

Mwet: A mute.

Myan: Mine.

Myell: Honey.

My-yea: To patch a trawl.

My-yee: Corn.

N

Naff: Nerves. Also, to have nerve; audacity.

Nah-jay: To swim.

Nah-veer: A ship.

Nair-veuh: Nervous.

Nan-yea: A spider.

Naught: Our; belonging to us.

Nawm: A name.

Nawm-bree: The naval; the bellybutton.

Nawss: A wedding.

Nay: The nose.

Nay-say-sair: Necessary.

Nay-twoy: To clean.

Nay-twoy-yea: Cleaned.

Nee-zawt: We; us.

Neg: An African-American man (often used as a negative connotation).
Also, an affectionate term for a young boy or male who is younger
than the speaker.

Neg-ress: An African-American woman (often used as a negative
connotation).

Nick: A nest.

Nick-de-gep: A wasp nest.

Nish: A prank or trick played on someone.

Noir: Dark; black.

Nonh: No. Also, a name.

Nonk: An uncle.

Noom-er-oh: A number.

Noo-vell: The news.

Noo-voe: New.

No-pote-tuh-kell: Anyone; anybody.

No-pote-tuh-key: Anything.
Nor: North.
No-vawm: November.
Nu: Nude; naked; without clothes.
Nuff: Is new; was new. Also, the number nine.
Nuh-nan: Godmother.
Nu-pyea: Barefoot; without shoes.
Nwaw: A nut that screws onto a bolt.
Nwee: The night.
Nyess: Nice.

O

Oak-taub: October.
Oar-aye: The ear.
Oar-yea: A pillow.
Oat-aye: The toe.
Ob-sair-vay: Observed; watched.
Odd-yanh: Nothing.
Oh: Water.
Oh-blee-gay: Obligated.
Oh-blee-yea: Forgot.
Oh-bleii: To forget.
Oh-fair: An offer.
Oh-feece-yea: An officer; a policeman.
Oh-fiss: An office.
Oh-liv: An olive.
Ohm: A man.
Oh-man: To bring.
Ohm-nay: Brought.
Ohm-sonh: A hook (a fishing term).
Oh-pay-ray: Operated.
Oh-que-pay: Occupied.
Oh-rah-gonh: A hurricane; a storm.
Oh-rodge: A squall.
Oh-ronge: An orange. Also, the color orange.
Oh-see: Too. Also, in addition; additional.
Oh-steen-nay: Argued.
Oh-stin: To argue.

Oh-taum: The autumn; the fall.

Oh-tay: Took out.

Oh-tour: Around.

Oh-viff: Swollen and sore.

On-dee-ray: Seems like; apparently.

Onh-bah: Down the bayou.

Onh-bah-rah-say: Embarrassed.

Onh-bay-tay: Bothered; pestered.

Onh-bet: To bother; pester.

Onh-bross-say: Kissed. Also, embraced.

Onh-car: Again.

Onh-dar: Sleepy.

Onh-door-mee: Fell asleep.

Onh-fawn: A child; children.

Onh-fawn-dee-goss: An illegitimate child.

Onh-fawn-say (a nautical term): Stuck.

Onh-flay: Swollen; puffed up.

Onh-goad-dee: Numb.

Onh-gah-jay: Engaged; put into action. Also, to hire someone.

Onh-gray-say: Gained weight.

Onh-grew-shod: Something quickly put together in a rickety manner;
     a contraption.

Onh-hoe: Up the bayou.

Onh-kick-ploss: Somewhere; in what place?

Onh-lair: Up; to the top.

Onh-man: To bring.

Onh-mah-ray: Tied.

Onh-marr: To tie.

Onh-nod-yair: In back of; behind.

Onh-pan-turr: The same likeness; one person resembling another.

Onh-pawn-yea: Caught.

Onh-poul: A blister.

Onh-pray-tay: To lend; lent. Also, to borrow.

Onh-sawm: Together.

Onh-tair: To bury.

Onh-tair-mawn: A burial; a funeral.

Onh-tay-ray: Buried.

Onh-vee: An urge; a desire.
Onh-veet: To invite.
Onh-vee-tay: Invited.
Onh-vlaup: An envelope.
Onh-voll: To swallow.
Onh-voll-lay: Swallowed.
Onh-voy: To send.
Onh-voy-yea: Sent.
Onk: Ink. Also, an anchor.
Ont: Between.
Ont-day-yarr: Outside.
Ont-donh: Inside.
Ont-sue: Under.
On-wee-yont: Lonesome.
On-wee-yea: Was lonesome.
On-yonh: An onion.
Onze: The number eleven.
Ool-sair: Ulcers.
Oo-tee: A tool.
Oove-rodge: Work.
Osh-tay: Bought.
Ought: To take out. Also, they.
Ought-ruh-monh: Otherwise; or else.
Ox-see-daunt: An accident.

P

Pad: To lose.
Pad-du: Lost.
Pah: Not.
Pah-cawn: A pecan.
Pah-cawn-yea: A pecan tree.
Pah-chawm: A chamber pot; slop jar (used before indoor plumbing).
Pah-ee-see: Not here.
Pah-guy: A paddle.
Pah-kay: A pack.
Pah-la-bah: Not over there.
Pah-let: A propeller.
Pah-onh-sawm: Not together; separate.

Pah-pah: Can't.

Pahr: To leave.

Pah-rah-sall: An umbrella.

Pah-ranh: Godfather.

Pah-rawl: A word.

Pah-ray: Ready.

Pah-ray-suh: A lazy male.

Pah-ray-suzz: A lazy female.

Pah-ree: To bet.

Pah-ress: Laziness.

Pah-roan: Parents.

Pah-rod: A parade.

Pah-say: Passed. Also, the past.

Pah-tah-lonh: Pants; trousers.

Pah-tah-sah: A perch (a type of fish); bream.

Pah-tee: To suffer.

Pah-tirr: Suffered; suffering.

Pah-tot: A potato.

Pah-tot-deuce: A sweet potato.

Pair: Daddy; father.

Pair-mee: A permit.

Pair-mee-syawn: Permission.

Pair-sawn: A person; someone.

Pair-say: To pierce.

Panh: Bread.

Panh-pad-du: French toast (literally, lost bread).

Pan-say: Pinched.

Panse: A pincer; claw.

Pan-sow: A paint brush.

Pant: A tin cup.

Pant-tour: Paint.

Pan-tour-ray: Painted; painting.

Par-donh: To pardon; to forgive.

Par-donh-nay: Pardoned; forgave.

Part: To carry.

Pauve: Poor.

Pauve-bet: "Oh you poor thing."

Pawm: An apple.

Pawm-duh-tair: A potato (literally, "an apple of the earth").

Pawmp: A pump; pumping.

Pawn: To hang; hanging.

Pawn-duel: A clock.

Pawn-say: Thought.

Pawnse: To think.

Pawnsh: To lean.

Pawn-shay: Leaned; leaning.

Pawn-yea: A basket; a bushel.

Pawn-yea-ah-lange: A clothes basket.

Pawp: A soda pop; a soft drink.

Pawsh: A pocket.

Pawt: A door. Also, to wear.

Pawt-mawn-nay: A pocket book; billfold.

Pay-shay: A sin. Also, fishing.

Pay-shurr: A sinner. Also, a fisherman.

Pay-tard: The posterior; the butt.

Pay-tet: Maybe; perhaps.

Pay-yea: Paid; will pay.

Pay-zay: Weighed. Also, pressed.

Peace-tosh: Peanuts.

Peace-tow-lay: A pistol; a gun.

Peak-urr: A picker; a splinter.

Pee-cawnt: Spicy.

Pee-cawt: The chicken pox.

Pee-chay: Shame.

Peed-row: A complicated Cajun card game.

Pee-jonh: A pigeon.

Pee-kay: A picket. Also, to stick or pick. Also, slang for intercourse.

Peek-onh: A splinter.

Pee-ko-shay: To pick for trouble.

Pee-lee-conh: A pelican.

Pee-nee-tawnce: A penance.

Pee-neul: A pill.

Pee-rouge: A pirogue.

Pee-say: To trickle out in a steady stream. Also, to urinated.

Pee-sue: A rubber sheet between the mattress and sheet to keep the mattress from getting wet when a child wets the bed.

Pee-tee: Little; small. Also, a child.

Pee-toe: Rather than; instead of.

Peev-yea: A chicken coop.

Pell: A shovel.

Pesh: To fish. Also, a peach.

Pet: To expel gas; a stinker.

Pezz: To weigh. Also, to press against.

Pip: A pipe for smoking.

Plan: Full. Also, pregnant.

Planh: Plenty.

Plan-yea: To complain; complained.

Plaut: A ball. Also, the occupants of the male scrotum.

Plawnge: To dive; to plunge.

Plawn-jay: Dove; plunged.

Plawnsh: A plank.

Plawn-shay: A floor.

Plawnt: To plant; a plant.

Plawn-tay: Planted.

Play-zear: Pleasure.

Plea: A flounder.

Pleu-bawn: Better (literally, more good).

Pleurr: To cry.

Pleuss: More.

Pleuz-yurr: Many.

Plock-men: A persimmon.

Plog: A plug; to plug.

Plonh: Lead.

Ploss: A place; to place.

Plot: Flat. Also, shallow.

Ploy: To fold.

Ploy-yea: Folded.

Plurr: To cry.

Plurr-ray: Cried.

Pock: A pen for animals. Also, Easter.

Pock-ah-ko-shonh: A pigpen.

Pock-on: A pecan.

Pock-on-yea: A pecan tree.

Pod-duh-an-fwaw: At one time; in the past; once.

Pod-duh-sue: On top.

Pod-duh-yair: After someone; chasing.

Podge: A page.

Pod-nah: A partner; buddy.

Poe: The skin.

Poe-lee: Polite.

Poe-mort: Dandruff (literally, dead skin).

Poe-ten: Blackberry dumplings.

Poe-toe: A post; a pole.

Poll: To talk. Also, pale.

Poll-lay: Talked; talking.

Pome: An apple.

Pome-duh-tair: A potato.

Ponno: The hatch cover for the compartment where shrimp are iced on a shrimp boat.

Pood: Powder.

Pood-ah-la-vay: Washing powder.

Pool: A chicken.

Pool-doe: A type of duck characterized by their white beaks and their diving habits to escape danger (literally a duck of the water).

Poo-lee: A pulley.

Poo-lye-yea: A chicken yard.

Poon-tang: Slang for intercourse.

Poo-ree: Rotten; decayed.

Poos: To grow. Also, to push. Also, a thumb. Also, an inch.

Poo-say: Grew. Also, pushed.

Poos-yair: Dust.

Poo-vay: Could.

Poo-war: Power.

Pop-ee-yawn: A butterfly.

Pope-yair: Butterfly nets (that skim the top of the water to catch shrimp as they travel with the currents at night).

Pope-yair-urr: One who uses butterfly nets.

Pop-yade-torsh: Toilet paper (literally paper to wipe).

Pop-yea: Paper. Also, a newspaper.

Port-tay: Carried.

Port-thray: A picture; a photograph; a painting.

Poss: To pass; a pass.

Poss-say: Passed.

Poss-kuh: Because.

Pot: The foot.

Pot-ah-lonh: A pants; trouser.

Pot-air: On the floor; down.

Pot-chanh: Belonging to.

Pot-tea: Left; gone.

Pot-tee-cool-yea: Particular; finicky.

Pot-too: All over; everywhere.

Prawm-mee: Promised.

Prawm-nay: To visit; to promenade.

Prawm-nod: Visited; visiting; promenading.

Prawm-yair: Is first.

Prawm-yea: Was first; ahead of the rest.

Prawn: Got caught.

Prawp: To be clean.

Prawsh: Almost; nearly.

Pray: To be close; near.

Pray-shay: Preached; preaching.

Pray-tawn-du: Someone engaged to get married.

Pree: Stuck. Also, price. Also, took; taken.

Pree-yair: A prayer.

Pree-yea: Prayed.

Pree-zawn: A prison.

Pree-zawn-yea: A prisoner.

Prett: A priest.

Pro-fay-surr: A professor.

Pro-feet: To profit.

Pro-fee-tay: Profited.

Pronh: To take.

Pro-pyea-tay: Property.

Pro-shan: The next one; the following one.

Pro-teck-tay: Protected.

Pue: To stink.

Puh-pair: Grandfather.

Pu-near: Will punish.

Pu-nee: To punish; punishing.

Purr: Scared; afraid.

Puss: A flea.

Pu-tanh: A whore; a prostitute.

Pwant: A point; pointed.

Pwan-tay: Was pointed.

Pwarr: A pear.

Pwauve: Black pepper.

Pwaw: Weight.

Pwaw-sawn: A fish.

Pwaw-sawn-rouge: A red fish.

Pwaw-zawn: Poison.

Pwaw-zawn-nay: Poisoned.

Pway: Stunk; smelled bad.

Pwee: The rain.

Pwell: A hair.

Pwell-ooze: Hairy.

Pyair: A kidney stone.

Pyea: The foot. Also, a foot, (unit of measure).

Pyedge: A trap.

Pyedge-jurr: A trapper.

Pyess: Each; one apiece.

Q

Quanh: A corner.

Quan-say: Pinched; squeezed.

Quanse: To pinch; to squeeze.

Quee: Cooked.

Queer: To cook; cooking.

Quee-zin: The kitchen.

Quett: A quilt.

Quiss: A thigh.

Quiv: Copper.

R

Race-pawn-sob: Responsible.

Rah: A rat.

Rah-boo-lay: Plowing.

Rah-fraud-deer: Got colder.

Rah-pawt: Report; to tattle.

Rah-pawt-tay: Reported; tattled.

Rah-pawt-turr: A reporter; tattler.

Rah-pell: To remember; to recall.

Rah-play: Remember; remembered; recalled.

Rah-sin: Roots.

Rah-teal-yea: False teeth; dentures.

Rah-toe: A rake.

Rah-vair. A roach.

Raub: A dress.

Rawl: To roll.

Rawm-plee: Fill; filled.

Rawm-pleer: Filling.

Rawn-cawnt: To meet.

Rawn-cawnt-thray: Met someone.

Rawn-flay: To snore; snored; snoring.

Rawn-sid: Rancid.

Rawnt: To enter.

Rawn-thray: Entered; came in.

Rawt: To belch.

Rawz: A rose. Also, a pinkish color.

Ray-can: A shark.

Ray-glay: Regular. Also, a shrimping term used to designate a dividing
of the shares; to settle up.

Ray-pawn: To answer; respond.

Ray-pawn-du: Answered; responding.

Ray-show: A heater.

Ray-show-fay: Heated; to reheat. Also, to get warmer.

Ray-vay-yea: Dreamed. Also, woke up.

Ray-zanh: A raisin.

Rear: Laughing.

Ree-doe: A curtain.

Reev-yair: A river.

Rell-monh: Really!

Redd: Stiff.

Ree: Rice. Also, to laugh.

Ress: To stay. Also, what is left over; remaining.

Rev: A dream.

Rish: Rich.

Roam-ah-say: Picked up; did put away.

Roam-ah-see: The debris left behind along a shoreline after the tide falls.

Roam-nay: Returned.

Roam-oss: To pick up; to put something away.

Rock-lay: To rake.

Rod-bwaw: A wood rat.

Roe-be-nay: A faucet; a spigot.

Roe-zoe: A lightweight bamboo used especially to make duck blinds to hunt from.

Ronh-yonh: The kidneys.

Roo: A wheel. Also, a flour sauce.

Roo-jawl: Measles.

Roo-lay: Rolled.

Roo-low: A roller.

Roo-vairt: Opened.

Roo-vair-tour: An opening.

Roove: To open.

Roo-yea: Rusted; rusty.

Rop-tee-say: Shrank; got smaller.

Rop-tiss: To shrink; to get smaller.

Rotten-war: A funnel.

Row-dye-yea: Visiting; riding around the neighborhood.

Row-tay: Belched.

Rozz: To shave.

Rozz-war: A razor.

Rozz-zay: Shaved.

Rue-see: To succeed.

S

Sah: That; that!

Sah-bin: A Sabine Indian. Also Sob (the current usage is derogatory).

Sahl: To be dirty; soiled.

Sah-lair: A salary.

Sah-laup: A messy female.

Sah-lay: Salty. Also, to soil.

Sah-lee: Dirtied; got dirty; will get dirty; soiled.

Sah-leer: Getting dirty; soiling.

Sah-lod: A salad.

Sah-teece-fay: Satisfied.

Sah-vah: "It goes" (an expression meaning that things are going fairly ok).

Sah-vonh: Soap.

Sah-war: Will know.

Said: Cedar.

Sair: To tighten. Also to serve.

Sair-cuy: A coffin.

Sair-pont: A snake.

Sair-vee: Served.

Sair-vell: The brain. Also, the mind.

Sair-viet: A dishtowel.

Samp: Simple; easy.

San-cont: The number fifty.

San-cont-soo: Fifty cents.

Sank: The number five.

Sand-soo: Five cents.

Sand-tour: A belt.

San-yea: Bled; bleeding.

Sauce-pee-cawnt: A spicy sauce made with alligator, turtle or fish; sauce piquant.

Sawm: A nap. Also, seems like; appears as though.

Sawm-dee: Saturday.

Sawn: His, hers.

Sawn-nay: Pealed; tolled; sounded.

Sawnt: To feel; to sense.

Sawn-tay: Smelled. Also, felt; sensed.

Sawt: To jump.

Say: It or it's.

Say-dye: Noise.

Say-poe-zay: Suppose; supposed.

Say-ray: Tight.

Says: The number sixteen.

Say-zawn: A season.

Schfawl: A horse.
Schfeuh: Hair.
Schmizz: A shirt.
Schmizz-daunt-soo: An undershirt.
Schocky-ann: Each one.
Schvoe: Horsepower.
Seck: Dry.
See: If! Also, to sit.
See-yell: The sky.
See-flay: A whistle; to whistle.
See-gahr: A cigar.
See-gah-ritt: A cigarette.
See-lan: A cylinder.
See-me-tyair: A cemetery.
Seen-yal: A signal.
Seen-yea: Signed.
See-tan: A cistern.
See-zoe: Scissors.
Seize-es-coll-anh: Seventy five cents.
Sell: Salt.
Sell-rhee: Celery.
Sept-tawm: September.
Sere: Sitting.
Set: The number seven.
Shah: A cat.
Shah-gree-nay: Chagrined; bothered.
Shah-lurr: Heat; stuffiness; warmth.
Shah-rett: A cart. Also, an old broken down car; a jalopy.
Shah-rod: A noisy carrying on; ruckus.
Shah-say: Hunted.
Shah-see: A window.
Shah-surr: Hunter.
Shah-wee: A raccoon.
Shan: An oak tree. Also, a chain.
Share: Dear; cherished. Also, high priced.
Share-pawnt: Doing carpentry work.
Share-pawn-tay: Did carpentry work.

Share-pawn-turr: A carpenter.
Share-shay: To go and get. Also to look for; search.
Sharr: A car.
Shaud: Was hot.
Shauf: To heat.
Shave-rett: Shrimp.
Shawk: To anger; to make mad.
Shawm: A room.
Shawm-ah-banh: The bathroom.
Shawm-ah-lee: A bedroom.
Shawm-my: A fight; an argument.
Shawm-my-yea: Fought; argued.
Shawmp: A field.
Shawnce: A chance.
Shawn-dell: A candle.
Shawn-dell-yea: A chandelier.
Shawnge: To change.
Shawn-jay: Changed.
Shawn-sonh: A song.
Shawnt: To sing.
Shawn-tay: Singing; sang.
Shawz: A thing; that thing right there.
Shay-riff: A sheriff.
Shay-say: Dried; drying.
Shee-fawn-war: A chest of drawers; a chiffonier.
Shee-kay: Chewed.
Sheem-nay: A chimney.
Sheen-waw: A Chinese.
Shess: To dry.
Shezz: A chair.
Shick: To chew.
Shiss: To be stingy; miserly.
Shock: One apiece; each one.
Shock-oh-la: Chocolate.
Shock-oh-tay: To whittle.
Shod-ronh: A thistle.
Shoe: Cabbage.

Shom-oh: A camel.

Shop: To drop.

Shop-ee-yawn: A mushroom.

Shop-lay: A rosary.

Shop-oh: A hat or cap.

Shoss: To hunt; the hunt. Also, to look for; search for.

Shot-tooi: To tickle.

Shot-too-yea: Tickled; tickling.

Shot-too-yuzz: To be ticklish.

Shouce: A stump.

Show: Hot.

Showed-yair: A cooking pot to be used in a fireplace; cauldron.

Show-kay: Angered; made mad.

Show-set: Socks for women.

Show-sonh: Socks for men.

Shwaw-zee: To choose.

Shyan: A female dog.

Shyanh: A male dog.

Sin: A sign.

Sin-dah-craw: The sign of the cross.

Sip: Cypress.

Sip-ree-yair: The swamp.

Sman: A week.

Sman-pah-say: Last week.

Sman-pro-shan: Next week.

Smott: Smart.

Soat-tee: Came out.

Sob: Short for a Sabine Indian (the current usage is derogatory, however). Also, a long eel-like silver fish.

Sock: A sack.

Socka-lay: A freshwater fish.

So-dah: Soda.

So-fah: A sofa; couch.

So-lem: Solemn.

So-lid: Solid.

Sonh: Without. Also, blood. Also, a hundred.

Sont: A saint.

Soo: Drunk.

Soo-coo: To shake.

Soo-coup: A saucer.

Soo-flay: To breathe.

Sook: Sugar.

Soo-lay: Getting drunk.

Soo-pay: Supper.

Soo-quay: Shook.

Soo-ree: A mouse.

Soo-see: The eyebrows.

Soo-vaunt: Often.

Soo-yea: Shoe; shoes.

Soul-dah: A soldier.

Sous-ronh: A nipple (for a baby's bottle).

Sow-siss: A sausage.

Sow-tay: Jumped.

Sow-vay: Saved.

Sow-vodge: A savage.

Sue-say: Sucked.

Sull: Alone; only; lone; single.

Sur-monh: Even; yet; still.

Sur-pree: Surprise; surprised.

Surr: Sister.

Suss: To suck.

Swaff: Thirsty.

Swain-yea: To watch over; to mind.

Swarr: The night.

Swaw-sont: The number sixty.

Swaw-sont-diss: The number seventy.

Swaw-sont-kanz: The number seventy-five.

Sway: Sweated; sweating.

Swee: To follow; following.

Sweer: Followed.

Swee-yea: Wiped clean.

Syan: Yours; belonging to you.

Syea: A saw.

Syoe: A bucket.

T

Tah-bah: Tobacco.

Tah-lurr: After while; in a short time.

Tah-pawsh: To hammer; to pound.

Tah-pay: Did hit.

Tah-pee: Linoleum.

Tair: Earth; a piece of land; dirt; soil.

Tair-mawm-ett: A thermometer.

Taunt: An aunt.

Taunt-kit: "You might as well." "You'd just as soon."

Taup: The top.

Tawm: To fall.

Tawm-bay: Fell.

Tawm-bow: A black drum (a kind of fish).

Tawm-ott: A tomato.

Tawn: Tender.

Tay: Tea.

Tay-rib: Terrible.

Tay-tay: Sucked.

Tay-ten: The breasts.

Tay-twaw: "Shut up."

Tee-boog: A little boy.

Teeg: A tiger.

Tee-kett: A ticket.

Teer: To shoot.

Tee-ray: Shot.

Teer-war: A drawer.

Teet: A little girl.

Tee-taunt: A little aunt.

Tee-yonh: A kerchief.

Tee-yoe: A pipe used for conducting gas or liquids.

Tet: The head.

Tet-durr: Hard head.

Tet-rouge: A redhead.

Thran: To drag.

Thran-nawss: A small, narrow canal used mostly by trappers.

Thran-nay: Dragged; dragging. Also, to crawl.

Thraw: The number three.

Thrawl: A thrawl.

Thrawn-kill: Quiet; silent; to be still.

Thray: Very much.

Thray-tay: Treated (for an illness or injury).

Thray-turr: A treater (usually an elderly man or woman who treats with herbs, salves and prayers (similar to the medicine men from the Indian tribes).

Three-yea: To pick through or separate (a term usually used to indicate separating the shrimp from the fish, crab and other trash on a shrimp boat).

Threff: Clover.

Thrett: To treat (for an illness or injury).

Threzz: The number thirteen.

Thrip: Gut.

Thriss: Awful; pitiful; woeful.

Thritt: A trout; green, speckled or white.

Thritt-vair: A bass.

Throm: To tremble; to shake.

Throm-blay: Trembled; shook.

Throm-my: A gill net; seine.

Throm-pay: Was wet.

Thront: The number thirty.

Throove: To find.

Throp: To catch.

Through: A hole.

Through-vay: Found.

Throw-lay: To trawl; trawling.

Tobb: A table.

Tob-lett: A tablet (to write in).

Tock-tock: Popcorn.

Tonh: Time.

Tonh-nair: Thunder.

Tonh-pet: A tempest; a bad squall.

Too: All; everything.

Too-jour: Still; yet.

Too-loo-loo: A hermit crab.

Tool-tonh: All the time; always.

Too-pay: Nerve; audacity; without shame.

Too-pot-too: All over.

Too-say: Coughed.

Toose: To cough.

Toosh: To touch.

Too-shay: Touched.

Toot: All; the entire thing.

Toot-sweet: Right away; now.

Top: To hit lightly.

Top-oh-shay: Nailing.

Tore-shay: Wiped (after using the commode).

Tore-tu: A turtle.

Tot: A pie.

Tour: A turn.

Tour-nah-viss: A screw driver.

Tour-nay: Turned.

Tow-row: A bull. Also, someone or something that is big and strong.

Tox: A tax.

Trah-fick: Traffic.

Trah-vie: To work.

Trah-vie-yea: Worked; working.

Trine-net: A small trawl used to test whether it pays to put the bigger trawls out; a test trawl.

Troad: Too many; too much.

Trock-ah: Troubles.

Trock-ah-say: Troubled; worried.

Troob: Trouble.

Trood-boo: A mud hole.

Tu: To kill.

Twaw: You.

Tway: Killed.

U

Udd-god: To look.

Udd-god-day: Looked; looking.

Udd-mawn: To ask.

Uff: An egg

Urr: An hour. Also, the time.

Uzz: To use.

Uzz-ought: Them; themselves.

V

Vah: To go. Also, will.

Vah-cawnce: A vacation.

Vah-ett: Will be.

Vah-fair: Will do.

Vah-liss: A suitcase; a valise.

Vah-lurr: Value; worth.

Vah-vitt: Speed (literally, "go fast").

Vair: A glass. Also, the color green. Also, a worm.

Vair-duh-gree: Mold.

Vair-nee: Varnish.

Vall: To steal; rob. Also, to fly.

Vanh: The number twenty. Also, wine.

Van-sank: The number twenty five.

Van-san-soo: Twenty five cents; a quarter.

Vaught: To vote. Also, your.

Vaum-me: To vomit; vomited; threw up.

Vaum-meer: Vomiting; throwing up.

Vaunt: the stomach.

Vaunt-ruh-dee: Friday.

Vawn: To sell.

Vawn-du: Sold.

Vawn-tay: Blew; windy.

Vawn-turr: One who tells big lies; a braggart.

Vawsh: A cow; female cattle.

Vay-ree-tay: Verity; the truth; honesty.

Vay-sell: Dishes.

Vay-yea: A wake for a deceased person. Also, a nighttime visit to a friend or relative's house.

Vee: Life.

Vee-day: To empty; to pour out.

Vee-lan: An ugly female.

Vee-lanh: An ugly male.

Vee-lodge: A small town (literally, a village).

Vee-neg: Vinegar.
Vee-pair: A viper.
Veer: To turn.
Veer-ray: Turned around.
Vee-rayed-boot: Changed ends; turned end for end.
Vee-say: Screwed.
Vee-zee-tay: Visited.
Vidd: To be empty.
Vie-yawn: A pretty female.
Vie-yawnh: A handsome male.
Vill: A city.
Vin-near: To return. Also, will come.
Viss: To screw (a screw or bolt).
Vitt: Was fast; speedy; quick. Also, a window pane, car window or other glass windows in general.
Voe: A calf. Also, a nephew.
Voe-lay: Stole; robbed. Also, flew.
Voe-lye: A fryer (chicken).
Voe-tay: Voted.
Vom-near: Will come.
Vonh: The wind.
Voo: You.
Voo-lay: Wanted.
Vott: Will.
Vray-monh: Really!
Vue: Saw; seen.
Vuff: A widower.
Vuv: A widow.
Vwaw: The voice.
Vyanh: To come.
Vyawl: Violet.
Vyawn: Meat.
Vyawn-moo-lay: Ground meat.
Vyoe-lay: Violet.
W
War: Will see.
Waw: To see.
Weh: Yes!

Whiss-kee: Whiskey.

Wit: The number eight. Also, an oyster.

Wooz-ought: Yall; you all.

Wrill: Oil.

Wrill-duh-see-lan: Motor oil (literally, oil for a cylinder).

Wuzz-anh: A neighbor.

Y

Yair: Yesterday.

Yair-oh-swarr: Last night.

You-zay: Used.

Z

Zabb: Grass.

Zanh: Tin.

Zanh-zanh: A kind of duck characterized by its awkward flight.

Zaup: A stupid person.

Zear: Nausea caused by something unsavory or distasteful.

Zee-rob: Messy; unsavory; distasteful.

Zell: Wings.

Zeuh: The eyes.

Zoo-tea: Tools.

Zwaw: A silly person (derived form "silly goose"). Also, a goose.

Zwaw-zoe: A bird.

Zwitt: Oysters.

ABOUT THE AUTHOR

For those who want to speak the old time Cajun French then you've come to the right place. The author was born on 9-11-46 during the "Baby Boomer" generation, and reared in a tiny fishing community named Dulac, which is a suburb of a slightly larger community named Grand Caillou, which is a suburb of a slightly larger town known as Houma, which is about 50 miles South of New Orleans. Where the communities end and the other one begins is anybody's guess. The Post Office knows, but it ain't saying. About 90% of the inhabitants are trappers, shrimpers, fishermen, crabbers or oyster harvesters. Most of the rest work in the many seafood processing plants.

The author attended Nicholls States University and obtained a degree in Psychology and attended Graduate School and is within a thesis of obtaining a Masters Degree. He also was drafted into the U.S. Army, where he got an all-expenses-paid vacation to Vietnam. He enjoyed his stay there, he tells me, except for those bombs and bullets flying around. It left him with an indelible mark on his psyche that time could never heal. It left him with a fresh perspective of what it meant to live in a free society. This book gave him some distraction from the experiences he faced there and a hobby that changed his life. Thus after about 40 years he has finally put the finishing touches to the book he has spent so long to develop, and it has now come to fruition.

The author has little publishing experience—with one book published but he has a wealthy repertoire of the Cajun Language. He entered a State Poetry Contest in the '70's and placed first in both categories and he netted a nice sum for his efforts. He also has three short stories (that's another story for another time) that were printed in The Courier, a daily newspaper, which has about 50,000 readership. I hope that he continues to try to write because he has an abundance of knowledge of his material.